Ethics in Public Life

Adapted from

Ethics, Conflicts, and Offices
A Guide for Local Officials

A. Fleming Bell, II

1998

INSTITUTE *of* GOVERNMENT
The University of North Carolina at Chapel Hill

THE INSTITUTE OF GOVERNMENT of The University of North Carolina at Chapel Hill is devoted to teaching, research, and consultation in state and local government.

Since 1931 the Institute has conducted schools and short courses for city, county, and state officials. Through monographs, guidebooks, bulletins, and periodicals, the research findings of the Institute are made available to public officials throughout the state.

Each day that the General Assembly is in session, the Institute's *Daily Bulletin* reports on the Assembly's activities for members of the legislature and other state and local officials who need to follow the course of legislation.

Over the years the Institute has served as the research agency for numerous study commissions of the state and local governments.

Michael R. Smith, DIRECTOR
Thomas H. Thornburg, ASSOCIATE DIRECTOR FOR PROGRAMS
Patricia A. Langelier, ASSOCIATE DIRECTOR FOR PLANNING AND OPERATIONS
Ann C. Simpson, ASSOCIATE DIRECTOR FOR DEVELOPMENT

FACULTY

Gregory S. Allison
Stephen Allred
David N. Ammons
A. Fleming Bell, II
Frayda S. Bluestein
Mark F. Botts
Joan G. Brannon
Anita R. Brown-Graham
William A. Campbell
Margaret S. Carlson
Stevens H. Clarke
Anne S. Davidson
Anne M. Dellinger

James C. Drennan
Richard D. Ducker
Robert L. Farb
Joseph S. Ferrell
Susan Leigh Flinspach
Milton S. Heath, Jr.
Cheryl Daniels Howell
Joseph E. Hunt
Kurt J. Jenne
Robert P. Joyce
David M. Lawrence
Charles D. Liner
Ben F. Loeb, Jr.

Janet Mason
Laurie L. Mesibov
Jill D. Moore
David W. Owens
John Rubin
John L. Saxon
John B. Stephens
A. John Vogt
Richard Whisnant
Gordon P. Whitaker
Michael L. Williamson
(on leave)

© 1998
Institute of Government
The University of North Carolina at Chapel Hill
∞ This publication is printed on permanent, acid-free paper in compliance with the North Carolina General Statutes.
Printed in the United States of America
10 09 08 07   5 4 3 2
ISBN-13: 978-1-56011-333-1
ISBN-10: 1-56011-333-2
☮ Printed on recycled paper
Cover design by Michael Brady

Contents

Acknowledgments   v
Introduction   vii

Chapter 1   Approaches to Ethics   3
What Is Ethics?   3
Ethics Based on Principles and Relationships   4
    The Deductive Approach   4
    The Inductive Approach   5
    Combining the Two Approaches   5
Justice and Caring   7
Questions for Reflection and Application   10

Chapter 2   Ethics and the Community   15
To What End?   15
Freedom, Rights, and Responsibility   17
The Rise of Individualism   19
What Citizens and Public Officials Expect of Each Other   20
    The Role and Responsibilities of Citizens   20
    The Role and Responsibilities of Public Officials   21
    What Do Citizens Expect of Public Officials?   22
    What Should Public Officials Expect of Citizens?   23
    Our Joint Expectations   24
Questions for Reflection and Application   26

Chapter 3   Ethics Codes and Regulations   33
Ethics Codes: Why?   33
    Certainty   34
    Accountability   35
    Identity   36
What Codes of Ethics Typically Cover   36
    Aspirational Codes   36
    Prohibitive Codes   37
    Hybrid Codes   37
    Which Approach Works Best?   37

Legal Limits on Ethics Codes   38
Creating an Ethical Climate: The Role of Codes   40
Questions for Reflection and Application   41

Appendix   Sample Codes of Ethics   47

Acknowledgments

About five years ago, I decided to embark on a new enterprise—the study of ethics and the place of ethical considerations in local government. I was not sure at the time where this endeavor would lead, but I was confident of my interest and of the potential importance of the subject for North Carolina's public officials.

While I was quite familiar with North Carolina's ethics-related laws, I also knew the limits of my knowledge in the field of ethics. To navigate successfully the waters on which I was about to embark, I needed guidance from more experienced sailors.

I decided to contact a former professor of mine, Dr. Thomas E. McCollough, associate professor of religion at Duke University. Dr. McCollough has taught and written in the area of ethics and public policy for many years. He graciously agreed to work with me, making suggestions for my research and serving as a gifted and thoughtful sounding board.

At about the same time I happened on the work of Michael Josephson, founder of the Joseph and Edna Josephson Institute of Ethics in Marina del Rey, California. Mr. Josephson, an attorney and former law school professor, has conducted ethics seminars across the country for a wide variety of groups, including public officials, students, and business leaders. The Josephson Institute publishes a regular newsletter and various other materials to help with the practical work of acting ethically in today's world. Mr. Josephson also gave graciously of his time and knowledge to help me in my endeavor.

My project was also aided substantially by John Sanders, then director of the Institute of Government, who supported my idea with a gift of that most precious of commodities, time. He graciously authorized a six-month special assignment for me to devote full time to my project, and he continued to support my work after I returned.

As I worked, I found much that I liked in Dr. McCollough's and Mr. Josephson's work. They both emphasize the relationships that exist between persons in our society, and the responsibilities that we have to the communities of which we are a part. Using similar themes, I developed teaching plans for several seminars, which I began to offer in late 1992. As is frequently the case, my classroom experiences helped me to further refine my ideas.

The approach to ethics that I take in *Ethics in Public Life* (which consists of portions of a longer work entitled *Ethics, Conflicts, and Offices: A Guide for Public Officials*) owes much to the guidance of Dr. McCollough and Mr. Josephson. It also benefits from the seasoning provided by the North Carolina public official students with whom I first explored the ideas there presented. I hope that my writing will be useful to them and to other local government officials as they consider ethical questions in the years ahead.

My own reflections on the subjects treated in this volume have also been aided considerably by the thoughtful suggestions of the persons who have reviewed portions of the manuscript. I thank Thomas McCollough and my Institute colleagues Stephen Allred, Frayda Bluestein, Joseph S. Ferrell, David M. Lawrence, Richard R. McMahon, David W. Owens, John L. Sanders, and Warren Jake Wicker for their many helpful insights and James B. Blackburn, III, of the North Carolina Association of County Commissioners for his assistance. I also thank the organizations noted in the appendix and their officials for permission to reproduce their codes of ethics. I am grateful as well to my editor Rebecca Johns-Danes, whose sensitive editing has been invaluable in helping the various parts of this project evolve into a coherent whole.

Finally, I thank my late mother, Ann; my wife, Meg; and my daughters—Rachel, Susannah, and Lucy—for putting up with me and sticking by me during the long years of bringing this work to fruition. To all of these persons go much of the credit for the result. Any mistakes and omissions are of course my responsibility.

Preserving the public's trust and pursuing the public good are never easy, but it is vital that we continue to do so if our democratic system is to survive and flourish. I hope that this book will serve for many years as a useful reference for public officials concerned about the ethical implications of their actions.

A. Fleming Bell, II
Professor of Public Law and Government

Chapel Hill, N.C.
Winter 1998

Introduction

A frequent recurrence to fundamental principles is
absolutely necessary to preserve the blessings of liberty.

Constitution of North Carolina, Article I, Section 35

Americans treasure freedom. The right to be and to do whatever we choose is important to us. We often see ourselves as independent individuals, intent on pursuing our own happiness in an increasingly impersonal society.

But this view of the world is not complete. We are also persons who live together in communities, communities with at least some shared history, traditions, and beliefs. We depend on the cooperation of others for the food we eat, the things we learn, the jobs we hold, and the love we share—in short, for much of what we need in our individual quests to live "a long and happy life."[1] We treasure independence and autonomy, but we also have common needs, common desires, and common goals.

How to draw lines between our public and private worlds is an issue that confronts local public officials daily. Most citizens recognize a need for local governments to exist, to help order our common lives. But many citizens also wish to restrict how much power the government has over them. We know that there must be rules, but we disagree about how much those rules should limit individual freedom. In short, what characteristics do we want our lives together to have? Where should individual freedom end and community responsibility begin?

The tension between individual and community responsibility also involves questions about the proper roles of the appointed and elected officials whom we have entrusted to administer public affairs and about our connections to them as citizens. There is a special relationship between the government and the governed in a democracy, a relationship built on trust. While we value freedom, we generally do not want our fellow citizens who work for us to take personal advantage of their public positions, nor do we wish to see favoritism shown to particular citizens at the expense of others.

The special relationship of trust between citizens and their public officials lies at the heart of this book. It explores what ethics and the public trust mean for our lives together, as well as ways that the ethical climate of government can be improved. By examining how ethics is applied in local government, we can clarify what we think about government, society, and the roles of individuals and communities. This volume is excerpted and adapted from a longer work that also covers conflict of interest and office-holding laws in North Carolina (*Ethics, Conflicts, and Offices: A Guide for Local Officials*).

Notes

1. Reynolds Price, *A Long and Happy Life* (New York: Atheneum, 1962). I am grateful to Thomas E. McCollough, associate professor of religion, Duke University, for suggesting the contrast between individuals in society and persons in community. His counsel has been invaluable in developing many of the ideas presented here.

. . . [A]s we move into the next century, into the new millenium, one of the great challenges we're going to have as a people is arriving at a set of values by which we will govern our relationships with each other as individuals and as nations.

The Honorable Robert W. Scott
Governor of North Carolina, 1969–73
Speaking at the North Carolina Association of
County Commissioners' 88th Annual Conference,
Pinehurst, North Carolina, August 25, 1995

Chapter 1

Approaches to Ethics

What Is Ethics?

People use terms such as "morals" and "ethics" in a variety of ways. One traditional understanding is that morality deals with questions of good and evil, right and wrong, and the like, and that ethics is the critical study of moral systems.[1] Nowadays, many of us use the term "ethics" when we wish to refer directly to questions of right and wrong, and it is this more common understanding of the term that we will follow in this text.

Questions of ethics are often understood as questions concerning the fundamental appropriateness (the "goodness" or "badness") of particular ideas or actions, and a person's ethical standards are seen as the standards of conduct that they follow. We say that a person is ethical if he or she behaves in ways that we think right or good. Similarly, a "code of ethics" is a set of rules that defines good and bad behavior in particular situations.

These three chapters will explore some general principles and ideas that many people have found useful in dealing with the questions of right and wrong that they encounter in public life. We will assert that public officials who must make real, practical decisions in real-life cases can be guided by principles that are agreed on by most of the community most of the time, and that they can make creative use of various approaches in resolving the ethical dilemmas that they face. Chapter 3 concludes with a consideration of ethics codes and regulations, and the role that they play in shaping the ethical climate within local government organizations.

We will not attempt here to resolve the quarrel over the meaning of terms such as good and bad. For thousands of years, philosophers have tried to define what is meant by "good." Whenever one has produced a definition with which he or she is satisfied, others have spent much time and energy poking logical holes in that explanation and offering their own solution in its place. In response to this quest, some philosophers have concluded that the entire enterprise of searching for the good is misguided and have offered detailed rationales for abandoning the attempt to find any common ground. Still others have reacted to this conclusion by pointing out the problems in systems that assume that good is a meaningless concept.

Our quest is more modest, our intended result more practical. These chapters' purpose is two-fold: to provide public officials with tools and approaches that they can use in their daily life and work, and to explore some of the principles that underlie the laws governing local public service that are commonly found in the United States and Canada.

Ethics Based on Principles and Relationships

When local government officials are confronted with hard choices about their personal behavior or about a policy or program, they sometimes say that they want to do what is right. By this they likely mean that they want to do what they consider appropriate, based on a set of fundamental principles or guidelines that they rely on to govern their behavior. And most public officials would like to think that the course that they are pursuing advances some notion of the public or common good: what will be best for the citizens and the society that they are called on to serve. The following are two approaches that can be used in evaluating situations from an ethical perspective.

The Deductive Approach

A principle-based approach to ethical decision making tends to be deductive, or *top down*. That is, one starts with a set of guiding principles that ethical persons should follow, such as honesty, loyalty, fairness, and compassion, and applies those principles to the particular situations that one confronts.

This list of principles used may be derived from any of several starting points. It may be based on one's concept of what is needed to achieve an ultimate goal, such as a flourishing or good life.[2] It may be derived from what one thinks is required by a higher authority or Supreme Being. Or, one may say that the list was developed for purely practical reasons: Following the listed principles helps a society function with a minimum of violence and other disruptions.

A public official can refer to such a set of principles whenever he or she is confronted with a question about the right thing to do in a particular situation. He or she may ask, for example, whether it would be honest to answer a citizen's question in a certain way, or whether adopting a certain procedure for distributing public funds to nonprofit agencies would be fair to all who would like to receive a grant.

If two or more of the principles conflict, the official must try to resolve the dilemma. He or she might set up some sort of hierarchy among the principles. Another approach would be to ask which course of action will produce the greatest good (an approach called utilitarianism).

The Inductive Approach

In recent years some writers have suggested that ethical decision making requires an additional dimension, a willingness to go beyond abstract principles to consider the people and organizations who will be affected by a decision and the relationships that exist among them. This approach is more inductive, working from the *bottom out*. One asks questions about one's duty or responsibility to others and about relationships that exist among the people involved. One then chooses the most responsible, caring option, without necessarily appealing directly to abstract principles such as honesty or loyalty.[3]

Consider again the earlier examples. A public official who wanted to emphasize this second dimension of ethical decision making would consider his responsibility toward the citizen who asked a question or the organizations that applied for public funds. He would also think more broadly about his relationship with the citizens he serves. What effect would concealing or revealing information, or granting or withholding funds based on certain criteria, have on these relationships? The official would try to solve the ethical problem in a responsible, caring manner. His solution would attempt to help, rather than hurt, important relationships.

Combining the Two Approaches

Most of us use both deductive and inductive approaches to some extent in our ethical decision making. For example, general principles such as honesty may be very important to us, but we are also concerned about and feel responsible to the people we serve. Indeed, we can directly link the two methods. If we prefer the top-down model, we may nevertheless say that caring and responsibility are two of our most important principles. If we like to approach things from the bottom out, we may still assert that a caring, responsible person tries to be honest, loyal, and fair.

Some helpful thoughts on combining the two approaches are provided by ethicist Thomas E. McCollough in a recent book. McCollough agrees that general principles such as liberty, equality, and justice are important as guides. However, he counsels that they should be understood not as abstract, formal ideas but as expressions of shared values, loyalties, and obligations to be applied in the context of the civic community in which we live.[4]

Combining our knowledge of principles with our understanding of how we are related to others, McCollough suggests that we should pose the ethical

question as, "What is my personal relation to what I know?" He explains that
we are persons who live in communities and whose lives require a moral context to be meaningful.[5] To McCollough, ethical principles are more than abstract
ideals or individual, private preferences. They are the shared and applied ideas
of people whose lives are interconnected.[6]

The assertion that our communities share ethical principles that we can apply to real dilemmas in a way that considers our relationships with others has
been tested by Michael Josephson, an attorney and founder of the Joseph and
Edna Josephson Institute for the Advancement of Ethics. In conducting hundreds
of seminars around the country, he has found surprising agreement among his
participants when asked to identify the characteristics of ethical persons. Josephson asserts that this "core of ethical values . . . transcend[s] cultures and time."[7]

Josephson currently lists six of these core values and principles. They are

- *trustworthiness*, including honesty (truthfulness, nondeception, and can-
  dor), integrity, promise keeping, and loyalty;
- *respect*;
- *responsibility*, including both accountability and the pursuit of excellence;
- *fairness*;
- *caring*;
- *civic virtue and citizenship*.[8]

While this model of ethical decision making is based on principles, it also
assumes that relationships must be considered. "All decisions must take into
account, and reflect a concern for, the interests and well-being of others."[9]
Those affected by one's decision are "stakeholders" in that decision. In a government decision, the stakeholders may include "a complex network of persons
and groups," including the persons directly or indirectly helped or harmed, the
person making the decision and his or her managers and coworkers, the governmental entity that the decision maker represents, and the government as a
whole.[10]

In this system, ethical values and principles always take precedence over
nonethical ones. The system attempts to solve the problem of conflicting principles that the top-down theory raises by appealing to both the decision-
maker's conscience and to utilitarian theory (the greatest good approach).
When two ethical principles conflict, the decision maker is to use his or her conscience to decide which principle is "more important under the circumstances."[11]

Josephson's ethics system is not without its difficulties. One of these is a
dilemma that confronts any principle-based approach to ethics: While persons
may well agree on broad principles, will they still agree when those general
rules must be made specific and applied to concrete situations? For example,
we may all agree that trustworthiness is important, but will we agree on what
it means to be trustworthy in a particular situation?

This difficulty is exacerbated because the system does not spell out an explicit goal for the ethical person to pursue. When ethical principles conflict, one must appeal, according to Josephson, to utilitarian theory and to conscience. But what end are we trying to achieve with this appeal? The flourishing of the individual decision maker? The good of the community? Truth? Upholding what is right? As McCollough points out, we need some notion of the common good and of our interconnectedness for a system of ethical principles to make sense.

Despite these difficulties, Josephson's work is very useful. He argues in a very practical way that there are fundamental principles on which we can rely as public officials to make decisions, and he has carefully identified a good number of these ideals. His work, like McCollough's, demonstrates that both the top-down and the bottom-out ways of thinking can be useful to public officials facing ethical questions and that they can complement each other in a mature person's thinking.[12]

Justice and Caring

In the previous section, we saw that deciding what is best or right can involve many different principles and at least two different approaches. Another helpful way to think about the ethical dilemmas that public officials face collapses those principles and approaches into an examination of two fundamental ideas—justice and caring.

The concept of justice has developed several meanings as it has evolved over time. To Plato, justice was the condition of harmony existing in a state between its members when each citizen played the particular role to which he or she was naturally suited.[13] Another ancient scheme divides justice into three types. *Distributive justice* is that done by the government in relation to the governed. *Commutative justice* involves the relationship of one person or group to another person or group, while *contributive justice* is that done by citizens in relation to the community as a whole and in service to its common good.[14] An old theological definition of justice is righteousness or observance of divine law.[15] A more recent definition picks up the same idea, defining justice as the quality of being (morally) just or righteous. Other related terms used to define justice include integrity and rectitude.[16] The modern philosopher John Rawls defines justice by asking what principles someone would develop to govern a society if one did not know what role or position one would occupy in it.[17] The legal world defines justice in terms of giving everyone his or her due.[18]

When citizens and public officials speak of justice as an ethical principle, they probably have in mind some notion of fair or impartial treatment. As Mortimer Adler puts it in describing distributive justice, equals are treated equally, and unequals are treated unequally in proportion to their inequality.[19]

We look to our federal and state constitutions to guarantee us equal protection and due process of law, and we expect that government officials will play a role in making sure that a "fair deal" is provided on an equal basis to all. Laws are passed, for example, that provide an opportunity to bid on public projects to all qualified persons who care to do so. And strict procedural rules are followed in granting public benefits, in hiring public employees, and in allowing variances from zoning ordinances.

Several other identifiable ethical principles have their root in, or are related to, justice or fairness. A person who is trying to treat others fairly, for example, will generally be honest and keep promises. By acting fairly, he or she shows respect for others.

Caring is another idea that has been important throughout the history of human relationships. When we think of caring, other words that may come to mind include benevolence, love, compassion, concern, and altruism. We recognize that there are many types of caring and loving; indeed, the ancient Greeks used several different words for love, depending on the context.[20] Love for God and for one's neighbor is a primary tenet of Judaism, Christianity, and other religions. Several recent books have explored the ways we care for one another as part of the process of developing a philosophy of caring.[21]

A caring public official might be defined as one who is attentive to the needs and desires of those whom he or she serves. After all, a large part of what government is about in a democracy is helping the people whose lives are affected by it and to whom it is responsible. Caring might be shown by providing a systematic way of resolving disputes through a court system or an alternative mechanism such as mediation; by maintaining the physical infrastructure of roads and utilities on which homes and businesses depend; by providing police protection; or by giving direct financial assistance to individuals in dire economic straits. One's view of the proper roles of local government will of course vary, depending on one's political philosophy. But nearly all of these roles involve some way in which all of us provide help to those of us who need it, so that our communities can be places where it is possible to live well, rather than simply to exist.

Caring, like justice, is closely related to other ethical principles. It is likely, for example, that a person who cares about others will show respect for them and will act in a trustworthy and responsible manner toward them.

The ideas of justice and caring roughly parallel the top-down and bottom-out approaches to ethics discussed earlier. To be just is to apply guiding principles impartially to particular situations—the top-down approach. Caring, on the other hand, suggests relationships: We care for, about, and with other people, and we ask what our responsibilities toward them may be—the bottom-out approach.

Justice and caring are also closely related to each other, as shown by one of the oldest ethical principles known: the Golden Rule.[22] "Do unto others as you would have them do unto you" suggests both that we should care about others and the effects of our actions on them and that we should treat each other fairly. Of course, the Golden Rule is not always easy to apply. Professor Warren Jake Wicker of the Institute of Government at The University of North Carolina in Chapel Hill, gives the following example. Suppose I am serving pie to you. I have apple and peach. I prefer apple and you prefer peach. Which do I give you? Apple, because that is the one I would have you offer me, or peach, because that is the one you like best, and I would have you serve me the one that I like best? And what should I serve to you if I do not know which you prefer? Of course, in this example I can ask your preference, but I may not always have the time or the means to do so. How does a public official determine what citizens prefer, for instance? In short, "doing right by other people" can sometimes be complex, even though we mean well. And it may require more information than we have available.

The effort to maintain a just and caring society sometimes seems to create conflicting situations. For example, most government officials can probably think of cases where playing strictly by the rules in order to be fair to all seems to show a lack of concern for the particular situation of an individual, a situation that is not explicitly recognized by the rules. But we also know of instances where bending the rules because of concern about one person's problem was seen as unfair by others who believed themselves to be similarly situated. This sort of difficulty may sometimes be solved by revising the rule in question, but not always.

To properly balance justice and caring, we need to consider them both when we confront an ethical dilemma. "Love tells us to care. But love works in a world of limited energy and limited money. You need a rule of justice to tell you whom to care for first, whom to care for most, and whom to leave to care for themselves."[23] Similarly, our ability to care may help to compensate for the fact that perfect justice is not possible in an imperfect world, where human beings often find themselves in a wide variety of difficult or complex situations.

Questions for Reflection and Application

For Reflection

1. What are some of the characteristics of the most ethical person you know?

2. Do you agree with Michael Josephson's list of ethical principles? What would you add to or subtract from it?

3. Do you think that we can analyze most ethical problems satisfactorily by asking, "What is the just or fair thing to do?" and, "What is the caring or loving response to this situation?" Are there other principles that are just as important? What are they?

For Application

Consider the discussion in this chapter about ethical principles and about the relationships between public officials and other persons as you examine the following case. Is there an approach to the problem that would be both just and caring?

THE DRINKING PROBLEM

Your best friend, Sam, has told you in confidence that he has a severe drinking problem. You have urged him to seek help, but so far he has not done so. You are a city purchasing agent, and you learn one day that Sam has applied for a job as a police officer with your municipality.

What action, if any, will you take concerning Sam's application? What principles will guide your decision? What effects will your decision have and on whom?

Think about the principles of caring and justice as you examine each of the following three cases. In each case, decide which principle you think is more important and why.

THE FILING DEADLINE

Jane Smith works for the county board of elections. Part of her job is to receive and process applications from persons filing to run for office. The filing period for the next local election ends at 5 P.M. on Friday.

At 5:02 P.M. that day, according to her watch, she is cleaning off her desk and preparing to go home when a breathless young man dashes through her door.

"Finally!" the young man exclaims. "Everyone in the courthouse has been giving me wrong directions! Your office is really hard to locate if you've never been here before. I'm here to file for county commissioner."

Should Jane allow the young man to file? What problems might Jane create if she allows him to file? If she does not? Where should she draw the line?

THE EXPIRED LICENSE

Tom Adams is a social worker in a rural county. A person comes to his office one Thursday who is badly malnourished and very poorly clothed. He would like to apply for the emergency relief that Tom's county offers. The county has a policy that anyone applying for emergency assistance must present a currently valid picture identification. The person before Tom produces a driver's license with his picture. However, on examining it, Tom discovers that it expired last week. The driver's license office in the county is only open on Wednesdays.

Should Tom accept the person's application or require him to come back in a few days after he gets a new license? Why?

THE LAST-MINUTE BID

Cindy Hayes is a purchasing agent for a large city. She is handling a bid opening for new police cars, which is scheduled for 2:00 P.M. in the sixth-floor conference room in city hall.

The wall clock strikes two and Cindy is about to begin opening the bids. Before she can do so, however, the sales manager for a large local car dealership bursts into the room with his bid under his arm. He explains that he arrived in the first-floor lobby at the same time (1:45 P.M.) as the other dealers who came to the bid opening. Because the elevator was very crowded, he offered to let them go ahead and to stay behind and catch the next elevator. Unfortunately, the next elevator didn't come for nearly fifteen minutes.

Representatives of all the other dealers who submitted bids are present for the opening, and they confirm his story. They all agree that they have no objection to allowing his bid to be submitted.

Should Cindy consider the bid? Why or why not? Suppose Cindy looked at her watch as the dealer came through the door, and it said 1:59 P.M. Should her response to this ethical dilemma depend on which timepiece she believes?

Notes

I am indebted for many of the ideas in chapters 1 and 2 to Thomas E. McCollough, associate professor of religion, Duke University, and author of *The Moral Imagination and Public Life: Raising the Ethical Question* (Chatham, N.J.: Chatham House Publishers, Inc., 1991). His written and personal guidance were invaluable as I examined the nature of ethical decision making by local government officials.

1. Much academic writing on the subject of ethics involves the systematic examination of particular schemes for answering these fundamental questions.

2. Such a goal is sometimes called a *telos*, a Greek word meaning end, purpose, or ultimate object or aim.

3. Variations of this approach are followed by Nel Noddings in *Caring: A Feminine Approach to Ethics and Moral Education* (Berkeley and Los Angeles: The University of California Press, 1984), and Carol Gilligan in *In a Different Voice: Psychological Theory and Women's Development* (Cambridge, Mass.: Harvard University Press, 1982).

4. *See* McCollough, *The Moral Imagination and Public Life*, 7–9 and 19–20.

5. McCollough, *The Moral Imagination and Public Life*, 28.

6. *See generally* McCollough, *The Moral Imagination and Public Life*, 46–59.

7. Michael Josephson, *Power, Politics and Ethics: Ethical Obligations and Opportunities of Government Service*, 3d ed. (Marina del Rey, Calif.: The Joseph and Edna Josephson Institute for the Advancement of Ethics, 1989), 1.

8. Presentation by Michael Josephson at Duke University, Feb. 10, 1993. For a detailed description of the various ideas embodied in each principle, see Josephson, *Power, Politics and Ethics*, 2.

9. Josephson, *Power, Politics and Ethics*, 13.

10. *Id.*

11. *Id.*

12. This notion parallels Carol Gilligan's idea that an ethic of rights (similar to the top-down approach) and an ethic of responsibility (the bottom-out approach) complement each other in a mature person. Gilligan, *In a Different Voice*, 164–65. See also the section of this chapter, "Justice and Caring."

13. Plato, *The Republic of Plato*, trans. Francis MacDonald Cornford (London, Oxford, and New York: Oxford University Press, 1945), 128–29 (from Plato's book iv, 433–34).

14. Mortimer Adler, *We Hold These Truths* (New York: Macmillan Publishing Co., 1987), 98–99.

15. *Oxford English Dictionary*, vol. VIII, s. v. "justice," definition I.2.

16. *Id.*, definition I.1.

17. John Rawls, *The Theory of Justice* (Cambridge, Mass.: Harvard University Press, 1971).

18. *See* BLACK'S LAW DICTIONARY (6th ed. 1990), s. v. "justice." See also definition II.4. of "justice" in the *Oxford English Dictionary*, defining justice in terms of judicial administration

of law or equity: "Exercise of authority or power in maintenance of right; vindication of right by assignment or reward or punishment; requital of desert."

19. Adler, *We Hold These Truths*, 100.

20. *See, e.g.*, Gregory Vlastos, "The Individual as an Object of Love in Plato," in *Eros, Agape and Philia: Readings in the Philosophy of Love*, ed. Alan Soble (New York: Paragon House, 1989), 96–97.

21. In addition to the books cited in note 3, *see* Debra Shogan, *Care and Moral Motivation*, Monograph Series/20 (Toronto: OISE Press, 1988).

22. Michael Josephson attributes versions of this rule to Confucius (500 B.C.), Aristotle (325 B.C.), the Mahabharata (150 B.C.), and the New Testament (75 A.D.). Materials from Michael Josephson, "Ethics Awareness Seminar Materials" in *Ethics Corps: A Training Program on Teaching Ethics in the '90s*, held Nov. 29–Dec. 2, 1993, Airlie, Va. (Marina del Rey, Calif.: Joseph and Edna Josephson Institute for the Advancement of Ethics, 1993), 27.

23. Lewis B. Smedes, *Choices: Making Right Decisions in a Complex World* (San Francisco: Harper & Row, 1986), 56.

Chapter 2

Ethics and the Community

To What End?

In Chapter 1, we talked about the characteristics of ethical people and about several ways of evaluating and solving ethical dilemmas. At this point, the skeptical reader may be wondering about the point of the exercise. How is it possible to resolve ethical quandaries in the face of so many different approaches? Is such analysis really worth its while?

If we adopt a view of the world that asserts that there is really no such thing as a principle and that everything depends on its context, or if we accept the view that our decisions about what is right or wrong are completely a matter of individual preference, we may well conclude that the entire project is impossible and a waste of time.[1]

To a practical public official, however, subscribing to such viewpoints is an unproductive and deceptively simple way of dealing with real, complex problems and issues. It is a red herring that will not work. In their everyday lives, people *do* act according to principles and they do judge their behavior and that of their public officials. Further, as Michael Josephson's work shows, people are able to articulate and agree on what many of these principles are. People do not simply go their own way, making light of the ethical dilemmas that they confront; rather, as we discussed earlier, they seriously apply both deductive (top-down) and inductive (bottom-out) methods to make sense of such questions. They further consider the impact of relationships and the roles of justice and caring in solving ethical dilemmas.

The early Greeks used the word *telos* when they sought to describe why it was necessary to pursue ethical questioning. A telos is an end, a goal, or a purpose toward which other things point.[2] When the Greeks asked what was good or bad, what was ethical or unethical, it was because they were seeking to draw closer to their vision of a good person or a good society. They called this vision the telos.

The noted philosopher Alasdair MacIntyre asserts that much of the confusion and battling about ethical questions seen in our society today is the result of our loss of such a vision. When we have no notion of what end particular principles or moral qualities point to, we are unable to order or apply them. We become like a body of disparate parts that has lost its head. MacIntyre is pessimistic about our situation; he doubts that we will ever regain a telos for our society.[3]

Public officials can learn much from MacIntyre's view of the problem, but there is no point to their roles if they accept his idea that a solution is not possible. If we do not think that we can make the future better, why do we bother to do the work of public service?

The late Stephen Bailey, a noted teacher of public administration, once observed that optimism is an essential characteristic of public officials. "Without optimism on the part of the public servants, the political function cannot be performed. There is no incentive to create policies to better the condition of mankind if the quality of human life is in fact unviable, and if mankind is in any case unworthy of the trouble. . . . Government without the leavening of optimistic public servants quickly becomes a cynical game of manipulation, personal aggrandizement, and parasitic security. The ultimate corruption of free government comes not from the hopelessly venal but from the persistently cynical. . . . [T]rue optimism is the affirmation of the worth of taking risks. It is not a belief in sure things; it is the capacity to see the possibilities for good in the uncertain, the ambiguous, and the inscrutable."[4]

So then we turn to the question of an end, a vision, for each of our communities. Imagine the construction of a building. If we can agree as public officials and as citizens generally on what we want our public structure to look like, then we are better able to select the bricks that we will need to construct it. The bricks are the ethical characteristics that we have been discussing. The mortar is the way those characteristics are tied together and applied, including considering the effects that our decisions will have on others.

How does a community develop such a vision? There is no easy answer, but it is clear that certain of the characteristics we have been discussing—for example, respect, honesty, fairness, and caring—will be important in the task. When we make ethical decisions as public officials, we do not simply make isolated individual choices. When we apply principles and consider relationships, we are acknowledging our connections with each other.

And we will need to continue to take note of ethical considerations regularly as we move forward toward that vision. Ethical decision making requires that we apply principles and consider relationships both in choosing a vision on which we can agree, and in choosing the means that we will use to reach that goal.

Professor Wicker notes that people are sometimes condemned because their actions suggest that they believe that the end justifies the means, while in fact it is the case that the end *must* justify the means. He points out that there is no alternative—otherwise we have only means. Of course, there are undoubtedly some means that could not be justified by even the noblest of ends. We must regularly ask whether the means that we are using are justified by the end that we are seeking.

Freedom, Rights, and Responsibility

As part of their disputes over what is considered good, philosophers and others also struggle with various ideas of *what is good for a community*—what we sometimes refer to as the common good—and how what is good for all of us together relates to what is good for each of us as individuals. We see this struggle especially in the United States, where we attempt to define the community's good at the same time that we honor a tradition that individuals are free to pursue happiness as they choose. If we are to develop a vision for our communities, we must first be clear about the nature of our rights and responsibilities as community members.

Three concepts that are very important in understanding the relationship between individual good and the common good are freedom, rights, and responsibility.

When Americans speak of freedom, they often have in mind "freedom from" something, such as freedom from government intrusion into their private lives (the "right to be left alone" discussed by Justice Louis Brandeis),[5] or freedom from government regulation of our business endeavors. This negative view of freedom has at least two important characteristics: It emphasizes the individual person and it is concerned primarily with each person's ability to act independently of other persons. Protection of the individual is very important in this view of the nature of freedom. People are only free if their ability to make their own choices and their right to be treated fairly and humanely are assured.

Under this view, we speak a good deal about rights. As the word "right" is used here, what we commonly mean is a justifiable claim, on legal or moral grounds, to have or obtain something, or to act in a certain way. By right, we may also mean that which is due to someone by just claim, legal guarantees, or moral principles. Thus we say that someone has a right to say what they please, and we say that Americans have the right of freedom of speech.[6]

The guarantee of certain legal rights is a powerful and important theme in our society. A quick examination of the United States and North Carolina constitutions, for instance, shows many examples of provisions that were included or added to make certain that individuals would be free to carry on their day-to-day activities without undue governmental interference (see, for example, the provisions relating to freedom of speech and religion, search warrants, and protection of life, liberty, and property).[7] Other sections provide that the rights of citizens will be equally protected[8] and explicitly guarantee that certain rights, such as the right to vote, will not be abridged because of race,[9] sex,[10] failure to pay a tax,[11] or failure to own property.[12]

But focusing solely on the rights of individuals provides an incomplete picture of our society. Human beings are communal, not solitary, creatures, and they are dependent on each other in many ways. Indeed, even when I assert that I have the right to act freely and independently, I am assuming the existence of social structures that acknowledge my freedom and legal structures that protect it. We speak of rights and insist on the existence of rights in large part *because* we are trying to figure out how to live together in a community: We want to ensure that the rights we each assert will be respected by the rest of us.

To arrive at a more satisfactory view of freedom, we must balance the idea of "freedom from" with the idea of "freedom to." That is, free citizens are free to take responsible charge of their life together.[13]

According to the dictionary, responsibility, accountability, and obligation are related concepts.[14] If a person must account to a group, an organization, or another person for something—for example, money, the use of one's time, or one's actions—then we say that they are responsible for that for which they must account, and that they have an obligation to those to whom they must account.

In this view, the members of a society are in various ways responsible for, and accountable to, the other members. These obligations of individuals to take care of each other provide an important counterpoint to the freedom to be left alone. As Thomas McCollough puts it, "we are creatures of community who have obligations to others that have to be considered along with our own interests."[15]

The idea of combining freedom with responsibility was more commonly accepted in America's formative years than it is today. As noted by Robert Bellah and his colleagues in *Habits of the Heart*, a study of individualism and commitment in late-twentieth-century America, people who spoke of individual rights in the early days of the Republic assumed a backdrop of civic or religious responsibility. While Americans had "come loose" from the older social structures of Europe and certainly valued their freedom, they also assumed a community life. They "brought with them ideas of social obligation and group formation that disposed them to recreate in America structures of family, church, and polity that would continue, if in modified form, the texture of older European society."[16]

The Rise of Individualism

Concern for this traditional mooring lessened over the years, as individualism became a dominant theme. Gradually, people were persuaded that "every social obligation was vulnerable, every tie between individuals fragile." The idea eventually became widespread "that the individual is the only firm reality."[17]

As individualism has become the dominant way of thinking, people have become both less willing and less able to talk publicly about moral obligations to others. Both the idea and the language of commitment and of community have become increasingly foreign to us, at the same time that the term "self-interest" has helped to make selfishness respectable.[18]

Legal scholar Mary Ann Glendon points out that modern Americans speak far more often of individual rights than of responsibility to others. She contrasts our "rights talk" with the view of some other democratic nations, which more nearly balance rights and responsibilities. Some European legal systems not only see each person "as a free, self-determining individual," but also see the human person "as [a] being defined in part through relationships with others." Glendon notes that in these countries "[m]any rights are viewed as inseparable from corresponding responsibilities." Thus along with liberty and equality, we find solidarity or fraternity. "Personal values are regarded as higher than social values, but also as being rooted in them."[19]

We see examples in the constitutions of European states of social responsibilities being given the same status as individual freedoms. Glendon observes that "[i]n most nations of Western Europe, programs such as old-age pensions, national health insurance, and unemployment compensation enjoy constitutional protection on a par with that accorded to such individual rights as property and free speech."[20] Most post-1945 western European constitutions, as well as several international declarations, see the individual as having a social dimension and treat the family as a fundamental social unit.[21]

Glendon, McCollough, and Bellah all call on their readers to recognize the problems created for our life together when we talk only of individual wants and desires and forget the language of community involvement. As Glendon has remarked, "Our overblown rights rhetoric and our vision of the rights-bearer as an autonomous individual channel our thoughts away from what we have in common and focus them on what separates us. They draw us away from participation in public life and point us toward the maximization of private satisfactions."[22]

To regain the older view is to see rights and responsibility or accountability as complementary notions in understanding how human community works. In a mature view of human experience, moral development involves gaining both an understanding of responsibility and relationships and an understanding of rights and rules.[23]

In this mature view, citizens do not simply act independently, but hold each other accountable for what they say, know, and value.[24] They hold each other accountable for the public good—for what is necessary for persons to flourish and develop.[25]

What Citizens and Public Officials Expect of Each Other

What then does it mean to be an accountable or responsible public official or citizen? Responsibility, like rights, must be examined in context in order to grasp its meaning.

To apply the concepts of responsibility and accountability to public life, we must define the roles of citizen and public official. We must ask who it is that citizens and public officials are accountable to and for what. The answers to these questions should help in understanding the meaning of responsibility for each group.

The Role and Responsibilities of Citizens

In Plato's vision of the ideal city-state in ancient Greece, distinct roles are played by distinct categories of persons who are suited by nature to perform the tasks each role requires. Soldiers defend; rulers make decisions; and tradesmen, artisans, and farmers produce and sell necessary goods. One's role defines one's public and private life, and people do not shift from one role or order to another. Rather, "when each order . . . keeps to its own proper business in the commonwealth and does its own work, that is justice and what makes a just society."[26]

In American society, we do not make such rigid distinctions among categories of people and the roles they play. Further, we draw a distinction between our public and private lives that would be foreign to Plato.[27] Yet, despite these differences, we do retain the notion of a public role, one that is shared in our case by nearly all members of the community. We call it the role of citizen.

Citizens are, literally, the inhabitants of a city or town, especially those who are entitled to its rights and privileges.[28] As noted in the earlier discussion of justice, we are fond of saying that we aspire to treat all persons (or at least all citizens) equally "before the law"—that is, that they should all receive the same protections and have the same basic obligations. Among these basic obligations are usually listed jury and military service, payment of whatever taxes are legally imposed, obedience to other laws, and the right or duty to vote.

To whom are these obligations owed? Perhaps the easiest way to answer this question in a democracy is to fall back on some version of what is called *social contract theory*: We have in some sense contracted with each other to live together in a society, and we have an obligation to each other as members of this body politic to fulfill those obligations that have been mutually agreed on in this social contract. A more practical rationale for such mutual obligations, for those who would say that they never agreed to the contract, is one based on necessity: So complex is our modern society and so great is our interdependence in so many areas of life, from food provision to road maintenance to disposal of wastes to health care, that we must agree to some sort of system of mutual responsibility simply to survive.

Does the traditional list of legal responsibilities of citizens tell the whole story of our public obligations and accountability to each other in our community? Or are there other things that we owe each other? Remember our earlier discussion of important ethical principles. Not only *can* such principles reflect the shared values of our communities, as Thomas McCollough suggests, but in fact most Americans *probably do* agree on a list of such ideas—recall Michael Josephson's experience with persons from a wide range of places, occupations, and backgrounds who shared a core set of ethical principles.

If Josephson is right—if most people agree that honesty, caring, justice, and so on are important, even if they may disagree about the precise meaning of these terms in particular situations—then perhaps it is possible for citizens to agree to hold each other accountable for acting in accordance with such principles. Perhaps we can agree that we should be honest and fair with each other, for example, and perhaps we can agree that such honesty and fairness is a basic responsibility owed by citizens to each other. Indeed, Josephson suggests that this notion of accountability is itself one of the ethical principles on which most people agree.

The Role and Responsibilities of Public Officials

In a democracy, the voters elect some of their fellow citizens to hold public office. These elected officials in turn appoint other persons to work for or serve the public, and some of these public servants (for example, city and county managers) appoint still others. In what way, if any, are the duties and responsibilities of these officials different from those of citizens generally?

In his book *The Responsible Administrator*, Terry Cooper points out that "[a]ll who work for a government bear a dual obligation: they are responsible to serve the public and they are members of the public they are supposed to serve."[29] He notes that these "dual role characteristics" have an ethical significance. Public officials can be seen as acting in a fiduciary capacity: They are entrusted with the responsibility to act on behalf of their fellow citizens, and they are bound by an obligation to those citizens.

Cooper suggests that "[t]his bond of trust is maintained only if one acts within a public organization as a citizen with certain added responsibilities—as a citizen first, and secondarily as one citizen among others who agrees to do work on behalf of all."[30] Those who hold these dual roles are "the especially responsible citizens who are officials."[31]

What does it mean to be trusted to act on behalf of and in the best interest of all? By examining more closely the meaning of this specific type of trust, we can begin to understand why citizens might expect to hold public officials up to such high standards.

In his book *The Logic and Limits of Trust*, Bernard Barber suggests that at least two meanings of trust are important in understanding social relationships and systems. First, trust is "the expectation of technically competent role performance."[32] That is, citizens may trust public officials to perform competently in their jobs, making technically correct use of whatever expertise they may possess.

The second meaning of trust relates closely to the fiduciary role of public officials. Trust is "the expectation that some others in our social relationships have moral obligations and responsibility to demonstrate a special concern for other's interests above their own."[33] Citizens may trust public officials to look out for the public good, to be accountable for more than simply their own personal interests. It is largely this second expectation that may set public officials apart from other citizens. Their special responsibility may consist in the fact that they act as fiduciaries on behalf of the rest of us. This fiduciary responsibility, this concept of the public trust, is at the heart of many of the laws governing public officials' conduct and roles.

What Do Citizens Expect of Public Officials?

So far it has been suggested that as citizens in a democratic society we may agree that we have a responsibility to each other not only to fulfill our formal legal duties of voting, paying taxes, and the like, but also to act in accordance with some set of generally agreed-on ethical principles. We have also seen that we may impose special responsibilities on those of our number in whom we place our trust as elected or appointed public officials. What in particular do we expect of our public officials?

Small, informal surveys of municipal elected officials and municipal and county appointed officials in North Carolina indicate that officials think that their citizens expect a great deal of them. Elected officials state, for example, that their citizens expect them to recognize needs, take action, and to make decisions that provide for the citizens' best interests and that are well reasoned, informed, and responsible. Put another way, they are expected to protect the citizens' interests in a responsible and compassionate way. Yet, they are also expected to make the best decision that will please the majority. Elected officials report that citizens want them to be available, open minded, and fair; to listen to find out what constituents want; to provide fresh ideas; to be a strong voice; and to be good caretakers of the public's money and trust. They are to exercise sound business judgment in decisions and to provide the services they commit to.[34]

Appointed officials report that citizens expect both everything ("solve all problems") and nothing (one person stated that "they [citizens] don't want to know" what government is up to). Others report that citizens want more for less; that is, cost-effective, quality service, or maximum service at minimum or no cost. Service should be uninterrupted, and if things break, they should be fixed. Other expectations mentioned include competence, quality, honesty, high standards, integrity, fairness or equal treatment, openness, and respectful, courteous treatment. Citizens also expect sacrifice; they may want exceptions made for them; they want more choices for the money spent; and they may expect local government to provide a safety net for the community. They want their public officials to listen and be responsive to changing needs.[35]

In short, the officials surveyed seem to think that what citizens expect from their "especially responsible [fellow] citizens who are officials" is behavior that is generally in line with some of the "ethical person" characteristics that we have identified (trustworthiness, respect, responsibility, fairness, caring, civic virtue, and citizenship).

What Should Public Officials Expect of Citizens?

What about citizens' obligations to public officials? Are they free after voting and paying taxes simply to go home and let the especially responsible citizens take care of things? In a democracy, it has traditionally been expected that citizens will let their officials know what they think about the issues and problems of the day, both those that only affect them personally (for example, a proposed rezoning next to one's home) and larger matters of more general concern (for example, what should the county's policy be concerning watershed protection and encouragement of industrial development). It is also assumed that they will judge on election day how well their officials have responded to the needs and concerns of the community.

One view asserts that the obligation or responsibility of individual citizens to the government they have created ends at this point. Once they have made their views known, citizens are free (and even expected) to spend the rest of their time in the pursuit of their individual happiness, leaving most of the work of defining and enhancing the common good to those whom they have elected and to the elected officials' appointees. Proponents of this perspective often assert that most persons are apathetic about government anyway, so that it is best if the hard work of governing is left to elected officials and to the trained professionals whom they have hired to do the job.

In his article "Putting the Public Back into Politics," David Mathews answers that this limited view of the citizens' role assumes much less interest and ability to contribute than actually exists.[36] He asserts, based on the results of a recent study, that much of the supposed alienation from politics and government that exists has less to do with citizens' lack of interest in or feeling of responsibility to their communities than with their feeling that elected officials will not take them seriously or give them a meaningful part in the work of promoting the public good.[37]

The researchers for the study conducted focus groups with citizens around the country. They found, among other things, that citizens today are not apathetic, but rather that they feel impotent when it comes to politics. They feel excluded from the political process, unable to participate and make a difference. On the other hand, when citizens think that there is at least the possibility that they can change things, they are quite willing to participate in public life and to "define the problems before them; set common purposes for action; and make choices for moving ahead."[38]

While citizens certainly want to hold public officials, special interest groups, lobbyists, and others accountable for their actions, they also want as citizens to "be more than bystanders, merely confident that the game of politics is being played cleanly and in their interests."[39] People want to do more than vote—they want to participate in the political discussion in ways that go beyond the occasional public hearing. Citizens want accessible places "where they can learn and talk about issues facing them and their communities." They want public officials, the news media, and others to hear their comments, and they need to know that if they make the effort, there is at least a chance that they can help create change.[40]

Our Joint Expectations

If the study just discussed is correct, it suggests that public officials may need to develop a different way of thinking about their responsibilities and those of their fellow citizens. Rather than viewing citizens as "clients," to be dealt with according to impersonal, bureaucratic rules,[41] or seeing them as "customers" of the services that local government provides, public officials need to take community members seriously as fellow citizens with whom decisions are made mutually about what sort of government policies and practices will best serve the public good. To do this requires going beyond educating the public—an approach that many citizens regard as patronizing[42]—and beginning to help each other see that we must work *with* each other if our common problems are to be solved.[43] New possibilities can emerge when the public is included in policy making "not simply as individuals seeking their disparate interests" but as "participants in deliberation about what is good for society."[44]

Under such an approach, all of us, citizens and public officials, also have an added responsibility—to think and act as if the common good matters. Instead of asking to be left alone or requesting special favors or exceptions for ourselves at the same time that we insist on evenhanded treatment for everyone else,[45] we must learn to think about our responsibilities to our fellow citizens. To paraphrase John F. Kennedy, we must ask not what our communities can do for us, but what we can do for our communities.

And so we return to the idea of a telos, a vision, for each of our communities. What is needed to create and work toward such a vision is a commitment by all of us to take our public responsibilities seriously. Some would say that the social contract that we have undertaken as Americans goes beyond merely making an agreement based on necessity but involves something more—unity as citizens in pursuing certain ideals, ideals embodied in documents such as the United States Constitution and the Declaration of Independence,[46] and in the sort of ethical principles that we have been discussing.

One of these ideals is the expectation that our government will be responsive to and controlled by the governed.[47] To overcome the cynicism that both citizens and public officials often feel and to move beyond immediate self-interest to focus on the society that we would like to become, we must return to an emphasis on this principle. Only by doing so can we hope to reestablish the trust that binds our communities together. We must trust and expect that each of us will fulfill our public role, whether as citizen or as elected or appointed official, in a manner that is in keeping with those ideals such as accountability, fairness, caring, and respect on which we can agree.

Are citizens and public officials up to the challenge? As noted earlier, the *Citizens and Politics* study found that citizens are very interested in working on solving problems, even complex ones, if they can understand how they are affected by the issues involved and if they can find a handle to grab hold of.[48] And many public officials show daily, as they work with dedication despite relatively low pay and perhaps little respect, that they also are willing to do their part in creating the kinds of communities in which we wish to live.

⊨

Questions for Reflection and Application

For Reflection

1. What do the citizens of your community expect from their public officials?

2. What do the local government officials in your community expect from the citizens?

3. Do the citizens of your community trust their local government(s)? Should they?

4. What is the purpose of local government in your community? Is it only a service provider or something more? What goals is it striving toward?

5. If you are a public official, for whom do you work? The local government as an organization? The citizens?

6. Do you think that the citizens and the local government officials in your community share a common understanding of what would be good for the community? If not, how do their views differ?

For Application

Developing a shared vision of the common good is a difficult task, but it is only part of the job. Public officials must also apply this vision, as they understand it, when they make decisions affecting their citizens.

Budgeting Time

Each year when it was time for the town council of Straightaway to consider and adopt the annual budget, the council members faced a common dilemma. They wanted to know about their citizens' preferences concerning city services and the direction in which the city should be heading, but they found that almost no one came to the formal public hearing on the budget.

After some discussion of the issue, the council decided to try a new approach. Beginning in January, council members advertised their availability to civic clubs, church groups, and other organizations to talk about city government, listen to citizens' concerns and questions, and take ideas and suggestions back to the city manager and staff for their consideration in developing the budget.

These informal discussions got off to a slow start, but as word about them spread, more and more groups asked council members to make presentations, and a number of citizens began to show more interest in the town's business. In fact, several citizens became so interested that they began to attend council meetings and to call the manager regularly to express their concerns and ideas.

The manager, Keith Knowhow, has gone along with the council's idea, but privately he has been less than enthusiastic. He finds it difficult to carry out the council's current policies and procedures effectively when he is constantly fielding detailed questions and suggestions for changes in those policies from citizens.

Keith's ambivalence about citizen involvement has finally come to a head this spring as he works with individual departments to prepare their budgets. Several of the most vocal citizens have asked him for copies of the draft budgets that the departments have submitted before Keith has been able to mold them into the overall city budget proposal. They have also asked that Keith meet with them to discuss the draft budgets after they have had a chance to review them.

Keith realizes that the drafts may be public records. However, he is reluctant to share them because he worries about how they might be used. He is also not excited about involving people—whom he considers to be fairly obnoxious and opinionated—even more deeply in the city's budget process.

The mayor of Straightaway is one of the most ardent supporters of greater citizen involvement. She also greatly respects Keith's professionalism and ability. Imagine that the mayor calls Keith for a report on the overall progress of the citizen involvement initiative and that he speaks frankly with her about his concerns.

If you were the mayor, how would you reply to Keith? Is there a problem here that needs solving? If so, what is it? How should it be handled?

Analyze the role of trust in dealing with this situation. For example, the developing trust of Straightaway's citizens in the idea that their government wants to hear from them and the council's trust in Keith to do a good job as city manager.

WANTED: A "GOOD" EXPLANATION

Sandra Jackson serves as both the clerk and the public information officer for a county government. The board of county commissioners recently made a decision that proved to be very unpopular. At their next meeting, the commissioners voted (at a time when no other citizens or members of the press were in the room) to revise the draft minutes of the meeting where the decision was made, so that it will appear that a much less drastic action was taken. Sandra has always prided herself on the accuracy of her minutes, and she considers this change to be a deliberate lie that keeps the minutes from being "full and accurate." She knows, however, that legally the minutes are the board's, not hers, once they have been approved.

What are Sandra's ethical responsibilities in this situation as she seeks both to serve the board of commissioners and to promote the common good in her community? For example, how should she respond to a newspaper reporter who calls her with a question about the board's action? Should she respond differently if a citizen who is affected by the decision calls?

FLOODS, TAXES, AND THE PUBLIC GOOD

You are a city council member. For several years, there has been a worsening problem with flooding in the municipality that you serve. Runoff caused by extensive commercial development poses a regular, serious threat to residents in some of the poorest areas of your town. After one recent storm, several homes and small businesses in the area were flooded.

A new drainage system would help to correct the problem, but it would be costly. So far the voters (who do not include most of the residents of the affected areas) have adamantly resisted tax increases or bond issues for correcting the problem.

It is also an election year, and although you are not up for reelection, several of your fellow members are in serious danger of losing their seats. These members have already promised *not* to raise taxes, yet they would like to support the drainage proposal. Unfortunately, the project is estimated to cost $1 million to complete, but there is only $500,000 available in the town's bare-bones budget.

The council members who are up for reelection talk with you about an idea they have. The drainage work can be split easily into two distinct parts: one costing about $400,000 and the other, about $600,000. They propose soliciting bids and awarding contracts for the $400,000 part now. They will tell the citizens that they support improving drainage, but that they do not support raising taxes to do so. However, the members also tell you that if they are reelected, they plan to let contracts for the $600,000 part and that they are willing to raise taxes if necessary to pay for it.

What do you think of your colleagues' idea? Is it ever necessary to keep people in the dark in order to promote the public good?

Suppose you think (1) that the information you have as a council member gives you a clearer idea of what would be good for the community than most of your citizens have or (2) that it would be good for the city for your colleagues to be reelected. Should either of these considerations influence what you say or do about your colleagues' plans?

Notes

1. These two approaches are called, respectively, relativism and emotivism.

2. A telos is an "end, purpose, ultimate object or aim," *Oxford English Dictionary*, vol. XVII, s. v. "telos" or "the end term of a goal-directed process; esp., the Aristotelian final cause"; *Random House Dictionary of the English Language*, 2d ed., unabridged, s. v. "telos."

3. Alasdair C. MacIntyre, *After Virtue: A Study in Moral Theory*, 2d ed. (Notre Dame, Ind.: University of Notre Dame Press, 1984).

4. Stephen K. Bailey, "Ethics and the Public Service," in *Public Administration and Democracy—Essays in Honor of Paul H. Appleby*, ed. Roscoe C. Martin (Syracuse, N.Y.: Syracuse University Press, 1965), 293–94.

5. Olmstead v. United States, 277 U.S. 438, 478 (1928) (Brandeis, J., dissenting).

6. See, e.g., the first two definitions of "right" as a noun (definitions 19 and 20) in the *Random House Dictionary of the English Language*, 2d ed., unabridged, 1656, and definitions 7.a. and 9.a. of "right" in the *Oxford English Dictionary*, 2d ed., vol. XIII, 923. I am using "right" as a noun in its more common, day-to-day sense, rather than in the technical legal sense employed by writers such as Wesley Newcomb Hohfeld, whose classic article, "Some Fundamental Legal Conceptions as Applied in Judicial Reasoning," distinguishes carefully among rights, privileges, and duties [23 Yale L.J. 28 (1913)]. No doubt many of the "rights" of which we speak in late-twentieth-century America are actually "privileges" in Mr. Hohfeld's scheme.

7. U.S. Const. amends. I, IV, and V; N.C. Const. art. I, §§ 12, 13, 14, 19, and 20.

8. U.S. Const. amend. XIV, §§ 1 and 5; N.C. Const. art. I, § 19.

9. U.S. Const. amend. XV.

10. U.S. Const. amend. XIX.

11. U.S. Const. amend. XXIV.

12. N.C. Const. art. I, § 11.

13. Thomas E. McCollough, *The Moral Imagination and Public Life: Raising the Ethical Question* (Chatham, N.J.: Chatham House Publishers, Inc., 1991), 69–70; and the discussion of negative and positive freedom in Robert N. Bellah, *The Broken Covenant*, 2d ed. (Chicago: The University of Chicago Press, 1992), 151–52.

14. See, e.g., the first and second definitions of "responsible" in the *Random House Dictionary of the English Language*, 2d ed., unabridged, 1641, and definitions 1 and 3.a. in the *Oxford English Dictionary*, vol. XIII, 742. I am *not* speaking of responsibility in the sense in which that term is commonly used in the criminal law; that is, being morally accountable for one's actions or capable of rational conduct (*Oxford English Dictionary*); having a capacity for moral decisions and therefore accountable; capable of rational thought or action (*Random House Dictionary*).

15. McCollough, *The Moral Imagination and Public Life*, 71.

16. Robert N. Bellah et al., *Habits of the Heart—Individualism and Commitment in American Life* (New York: Harper & Row, 1985), 276.

17. *Id.*

18. McCollough, *The Moral Imagination and Public Life*, 73.

19. Mary Ann Glendon, *Rights Talk—The Impoverishment of Political Discourse* (New York: The Free Press, 1991), 161.

20. Glendon, *Rights Talk*, 99.

21. *Id.* at 73–74.

22. *Id.* at 143.

23. Carol Gilligan, *In a Different Voice: Psychological Theory and Women's Development* (Cambridge, Mass.: Harvard University Press, 1982), 19.

24. *Id.* at 77–79, 84–85.

25. McCollough, *The Moral Imagination and Public Life*, 79. Similarly, to Bellah and his colleagues, "The question for the responsible citizen today is, Are we responsible only for our own good or also for the common good? Even a benevolent tyranny can permit us the former; only a genuine democracy can make possible the latter." Robert N. Bellah et al., *The Good Society* (New York: Alfred A. Knopf, 1991), 81.

26. Plato, *The Republic of Plato*, trans. Francis MacDonald Cornford (London, Oxford, and New York: Oxford University Press, 1945), 129 (from Plato's book iv, 434). See generally 128–29.

27. *See* McCollough, *The Moral Imagination and Public Life*, 61–62.

28. See the main definitions of "citizen" in the *Oxford English Dictionary*, vol. III, 249–50, and in the *Random House Dictionary of the English Language*, 2d ed., unabridged, 377. A "citizen" may also be defined as a native or naturalized member of a state or nation who is entitled to its protection. Citizens owe allegiance to the government (*Random House Dictionary*) and have the privilege of voting for public offices (*Oxford English Dictionary*).

29. Terry L. Cooper, *The Responsible Administrator—An Approach to Ethics for the Administrative Role*, 3d ed. (San Francisco: Jossey-Bass Inc., Publishers, 1990), 40.

30. *Id.* at 41.

31. *Id.* at 41, quoting Paul Appleby.

32. Bernard Barber, *The Logic and Limits of Trust* (New Brunswick, N.J.: Rutgers University Press, 1983), 14.

33. *Id.*

34. Notes of author, listing responses to the question, "Name at least one thing that your citizens expect of you," by North Carolina municipal elected officials participating in seminar "Thinking About Ethics in City Government," sponsored by the Institute of Government, Asheville, N.C., April 29–30, 1993.

35. Notes of author, listing responses to the question, "What do citizens expect of you?" by members of the 1992–93 Municipal and County Administration II classes at the Institute of Government, February 17–18, 1993; and responses to the question "What do your citizens expect from their local government?" by members of the 1995–96 Municipal and County Administration II classes at the Institute of Government, November 8, 1995.

36. David Mathews, "NCR Focus: Putting the Public Back into Politics," *National Civic Review* 80 (Fall 1991): 343–51.

37. Mathews's comments are based on the results of a study, *Citizens and Politics: A View from Main Street America*. A report of the study's findings was prepared for the Kettering Foundation by the Harwood Group, Bethesda, Md. (Dayton, Ohio: Kettering Foundation, 1991).

38. Harwood Group, *Citizens and Politics*, 3–5.

39. *Id.* at 4.

40. *Id.* at 7.

41. See the discussion of the use of bureaucratic language in McCollough, *The Moral Imagination and Public Life*, 84–85.

42. Mathews, "NCR Focus": 345.

43. Mathews, "NCR Focus": 351.

44. McCollough, *The Moral Imagination and Public Life*, 88.

45. See the responses to questions about what citizens expect, summarized *supra* note 35.

46. *See generally* Bellah, *The Broken Covenant*, 151–52, *supra* note 13, and John A. Rohr, *Ethics for Bureaucrats: An Essay on Law and Values*, 2d ed. (New York: Marcel Dekker, 1989). Rohr's book is discussed briefly in the notes to the section in Chapter 3 on "Certainty." In this section, the author makes a case for using constitutional principles as ethical norms.

47. Mathews, "NCR Focus": 344. *Cf.* the Declaration of Independence ("to secure these Rights, Governments are instituted among Men, *deriving their just Powers from the Consent of the Governed* . . .") (emphasis added).

48. Mathews, "NCR Focus": 348–49.

Chapter 3

Ethics Codes and Regulations

How can a local government encourage its officials to behave in an ethical manner—to be aware of the public trust that they safeguard, and to follow standards of behavior that reflect concern for ethical principles and for the effects of their decisions on others? As part of the quest to improve ethical behavior, we sometimes turn not only to principles and methods such as those discussed in chapters 1 and 2 and to general laws passed by legislatures but also to written codes and regulations governing the conduct of officials in a particular jurisdiction or profession.

The content of such rules and standards varies widely. They may be very specific or very general. They may be concerned with a broad range of ethical issues, or they may focus on one specific issue, such as the personal financial interests of public officials. They may apply to one type of public servant, such as city or county managers, or to all the elected and/or appointed officials of a particular jurisdiction.

In this chapter all of these different types of written rules and standards will be referred to collectively as "ethics codes and regulations" or "ethics codes." We will look at why such rules are enacted, what they typically cover, and how they work. We will examine the possible consequences, both positive and negative, of a code-based approach to ethics. We will conclude by considering recommendations concerning the appropriate place of ethics codes in a program to promote a particular ethical climate at the local level.

Ethics Codes: Why?

We have seen that there are certain commonsense ethical principles and approaches that public officials can apply in deciding what to do when ethical dilemmas arise. States and provinces also have a variety of constitutional, statutory, and common-law provisions that supplement and support these principles and approaches by providing legal rules to guide public officials through many of the conflicts that they may encounter.

Given these principles, approaches, and laws, it seems fair to ask whether more is needed. Why do some local governments and professional groups feel that it is important to put in place additional bodies of rules to guide the conduct of their officials and members?

There are three main reasons for using ethics codes: *certainty, accountability,* and a desire to create an institutional or professional *identity.*[1]

Certainty

In our society, where differences in philosophies and perspectives are often emphasized more than similarities,[2] people who seek something on which they *can* agree will often focus on laws and other rules. Rules have the advantage of being definite. If they are well drafted, one can look at them and determine exactly what one can and cannot do and exactly what limits are imposed by the wider community. And if rules are arrived at through a process that is viewed as legitimate, some of them may help us define in more detail what a community would be like if it were involved in pursuing the common good.

Some constitutional principles, such as the requirements of equal protection and due process of law, function in our society basically as ethical norms, providing standards of good and bad against which we measure each other's conduct. Indeed, at least one noted teacher of ethics advocates using constitutional principles and the court decisions interpreting them as the foundation for teaching ethics to government officials.[3]

Perhaps because of our perceived differences and the importance that we attach to the law as a common denominator among us, many people look to legal processes to settle their disagreements rather than trying to work things out among themselves. This in turn contributes to the perceived importance of rules because the legal system itself is heavily rules oriented.

If we are a rule-oriented society with a rule-oriented system of government, as the plethora of laws and regulations that have been enacted in recent years suggests,[4] then it stands to reason that we might wish to know what our boundaries are in various situations where we interact with others. Codes of ethics can sometimes supply that definiteness, that sense of certainty and finality, that we desire. Codes help us to clarify the meaning of ethical behavior, to better understand the standard of conduct that goes beyond what the general law requires.

A concept related to certainty is fairness. It may be somewhat easier to treat people in an organization fairly if ethics rules and codes to which they are subject are written in clear, well-thought-out language. In return, those who are regulated can know, with some degree of certainty, what is permitted and what is not, and those who are charged with enforcement can more easily avoid charges of discrimination or excessive subjectivity. Of course, as we will discuss later and as many statute and rule drafters can attest, achieving such clarity and precision in an easily understandable document is often much easier said than done.

Ethics codes and regulations may also contribute to certainty by serving as "gap fillers." Codes are often specifically designed to deal with situations that general laws do not address. For example, Chapter 133, Section 32, of the North Carolina General Statutes (hereinafter G.S.), a statute regulating the giving and receiving of gifts and favors in connection with government contracting, states that it is not intended to prevent the giving and receiving of "advertising items or souvenirs of nominal value." But the statute does not specify what "nominal value" means. A code could provide some guidance in this area, even though in most North American jurisdictions the courts must ultimately decide the meaning of statutory terms.[5]

Accountability

Public officials are entrusted with work that is not merely their own but is done for the benefit of all persons in the community of which they are a part. As discussed in Chapter 2, this public trust requires that public officials be subjected to a high standard of accountability.

The specificity of many ethics codes and regulations may help to ensure that public officials are held accountable for the work that they do. Codes may go beyond the guidance provided by general ethical principles to answer specific questions and to impose verifiable standards that public officials must meet. Thus, for example, a code might not only acknowledge the importance of honesty but might specify various actions that will be considered dishonest.

Ethics codes for local governments and professional groups may function much like statewide laws dealing with conflicts of interest, gifts and favors, and the like. But because they are designed for a specific professional group or local jurisdiction, they can be tailored for specific situations and designed to address particular concerns. It is possible to impose a higher standard of accountability than is found in a general law by, for example, forbidding the receiving of any gifts, with no exception for items of nominal value.

Definite standards may also help public officials deal with difficult situations that they face. It may be easier, for example, to refuse a gift because an organization simply forbids receiving gifts, than to try to explain to a citizen why what he or she has offered is more than a nominal gift and must be declined.

On the other hand, the use of specific standards that supply easy answers may actually have a negative effect on accountability by giving public officials the freedom *not* to think carefully about situations that they encounter or to exercise good judgment. We will return to this idea later in this chapter.

Identity

Most people want to be thought of as ethical, as persons who do the right thing. Securing such an identity is especially important for groups of people who are expected to earn and keep the public's trust. Both professional groups of public officials, such as clerks or finance officers, as well as the officials of individual cities and counties may wish to be seen as upholding high ethical standards.

One way to increase a group's visibility and perhaps to help secure its identity as an ethical organization is to publish and follow a set of ethical standards. Following a code can help the elected and appointed officials of a local government build and maintain a positive ethical climate within their organization. An ethics code to which a professional group adheres provides a definition of what it means to be ethical within that profession and adds an important statewide or national perspective for members of that profession.

What Codes of Ethics Typically Cover

We noted earlier that ethics codes and regulations vary widely in scope. Codes typically come in two basic types, aspirational and prohibitive. Of course, variations between the two types are also possible.

Aspirational Codes

Aspirational codes are those that deal primarily with how we ought to be. They state the norms of behavior toward which we aspire. Such codes range from the general (see, for example, the Code of Ethics of the International Institute of Municipal Clerks [IIMC], reprinted in the Appendix) to the fairly specific (see, for example, the draft code of ethics of the North Carolina Association of County Commissioners and the Code of Ethics for [North Carolina] School Board Members, also reprinted in the Appendix).

Aspirational codes typically emphasize the same sorts of ethical principles that we discussed in Chapter 1. The IIMC Code, for example, speaks in various ways of trust and responsibility. Some of the key themes in the county commissioners' code are integrity, fairness, avoidance of conflicts of interest, and the need to act diligently and responsibly and to inspire and maintain public confidence and trust.

Aspirational codes appeal to humans' higher and better desires. They promote ethical behavior by challenging us to go beyond the letter of the law and to become the especially responsible citizens discussed in Chapter 2.

Prohibitive Codes

Prohibitive codes, in contrast, recognize that public officials may sometimes act in a manner that is self-serving or otherwise incompatible with the public trust that they have been given. They promote better behavior by prohibiting and specifying sanctions for conduct that is considered to be unethical.

Three examples of prohibitive codes are reprinted in the Appendix. The "Resolution of Intent" of the City of Washington, North Carolina (the third sample code of ethics), is intended primarily to prohibit public officials from using their public positions for private gain. It provides for investigations of alleged violations, for procedural due process for the alleged violator, and for sanctions up to and including termination for city employees. A council member who violates the resolution may be censured by the council.

Similarly, the Code of Ethics of the Triangle Transit Authority in North Carolina (the fourth sample code in the appendix) deals with conflicts of interest, gifts, incompatible service, and disclosure of financial information. It provides not only for investigation of alleged sanctions but also for the rendering of advisory opinions on ethics questions by the authority's attorney.

In the city of Hickory, North Carolina, ordinance provisions dealing with conflicts of interest involving city officials (included in the fifth set of sample materials) make heavy use of full disclosure as a means of handling ethical conflicts. The ordinance also provides for hearings, sanctions, and advisory opinions.

Hybrid Codes

Some codes combine aspirational features with prohibitions of certain acts. The International City/County Management Association's (ICMA) Code of Ethics with Guidelines and its accompanying Rules of Procedure for Enforcement (see appendix) together form a good example of such a combined approach. The code establishes high standards of conduct for city and county managers who are members of the association and imposes various sanctions, including expulsion from membership, for violations of the code's provisions.

Which Approach Works Best?

Is it better to praise and inspire, or to warn and sanction, when one wants to generate support by public officials for ethical principles? For many years public administration specialists have grappled with this question when examining whether public officials should be governed primarily by internal or by external controls.

The differences between internal and external controls are similar to the distinctions between aspirational and prohibitive codes. Internal controls are positive and aspirational. They "consist of values and ethical standards cultivated within each public servant" through training and professional socialization and are "intended to encourage ethical conduct in the absence of rules and monitoring systems." External controls, on the other hand, involve "attempts to impose on the conduct of individual public servants constraints that originate from outside themselves" through rules, laws, and changes in organizational structures.[6]

At their best, the two types of controls should balance and reinforce each other and not give conflicting signals. As Terry Cooper explains, "there must be enough control from outside the individual to discourage those inclinations toward indulgence of self-interest, but enough internal control to encourage the most socially constructive, idealistic, altruistic, and creative impulses to flourish."[7]

Michael Josephson, whose research concerning shared ethical principles was discussed in Chapter 1, defines several characteristics of an effective ethics code. According to Josephson, it should contain a statement of guiding principles that sets the tone for the code and to which public officials may return as they construe the more detailed code provisions. In effect, this is the aspirational part of the code.

But Josephson's ideal code also would have prohibitive aspects. That is, the code should specifically apply principles to situations that are reasonably likely to occur, and it should be comprehensive, covering the full range of ethical principles that apply to public officials. At the same time, however, the code should be realistic in the standard of behavior that it expects. It should be clear and unambiguous, simple, and easy to read and use, with devices such as indexes to help make it accessible. Finally, it should include a commentary with explanations and illustrations.[8]

Is it realistic to assume that a code embodying all of these characteristics can be drafted? Some of these qualities, such as comprehensiveness, simplicity, and ease of use, seem to point in contrary directions, even if they are not mutually exclusive.

The drafter of Josephson's ideal code will encounter an age-old problem in legal writing—how does one draft clearly and simply, with general enough language to cover a variety of situations and at the same time draft specifically enough to avoid uncertainty and to make it reasonably possible to adhere to the code's commands? Furthermore, if the code is being drafted for a local government, the writer must also consider the limits imposed on governmental codes of ethics by various other laws.

Legal Limits on Ethics Codes

It is clear that local governing bodies such as city councils and boards of county commissioners can regulate the conduct of their employees. They can do so by enforcing statutory and common-law rules in most cases and also by adopting local regulations that are stricter (but not more lenient) than these rules. Depending on the jurisdiction, local regulations may be included as part of personnel policies or ordinances[9] or in separate codes of ethics. To the extent that personnel rules and codes of ethics deal with matters relating to employees' job responsibilities and to their use of public property, they are well within the statutory authority of most public employers.

There is, however, an outer limit concerning the types of conduct which employers may regulate. Public employees do not completely give up their rights to freedom of speech and association when they go to work for the government. Thus while provisions in an ethics code that prohibit receiving gifts from contractors or making personal use of public property are clearly legal, provisions regulating whom employees can associate with, what organizations they can join, or what otherwise legal activities they can engage in off the job are generally constitutionally suspect, at least in the United States.[10] Such rules are legally defensible only if they relate in some direct way to workplace performance. Thus, for example, while a public employer cannot prohibit off-the-job drinking, it can forbid employees to come to work drunk.

A public governing board also may have very little ability to regulate the conduct of its own members. Members of city councils and boards of county commissioners, for example, generally receive their seats and legal powers through actions of the state legislature and the voters. Although laws vary, in many jurisdictions each of the members is a legally independent actor, subject only to minimal control by the others. Unlike a self-governing private organization, which was created by persons who became its members and continues to exist under its members' control, the members of a local governing board are often given no general authority to discipline each other. At most, the board in such a jurisdiction can register its displeasure with a member's conduct by adopting a nonbinding resolution censuring the member.

What about ethics codes that apply to persons other than employees or governing board members, such as members of appointed boards of the local government or relatives of employees or board members? If a local governing board has authority to create another board or committee, it probably has power to prescribe ethics regulations applicable to members of that board, much as it can prescribe regulations for its employees.[11] But its ability to regulate the conduct of ordinary citizens who are neither public officials nor employees and who do not serve on government boards is much more limited.

Ethics codes and regulations generally do not apply to persons not connected with the local government unless they are adopted as police-power ordinances[12] by a local government with general ordinance-making power.[13] City and county ordinances relating to ethics, like other ordinances, must be consistent with higher laws such as state and federal constitutions, statutes, and regulations.[14] Thus, for example, a restriction forbidding relatives of governing board members or of government employees to bid on public con-

struction contracts would be legally suspect in North Carolina. Such an ordinance would be inconsistent with the general requirement for open public
competition that underlies North Carolina's competitive-bidding statutes.

Creating an Ethical Climate: The Role of Codes

The difficulty of drafting and interpreting codes of ethics and the limits on
their enforceability should not blind us to the potential advantages of using
codes to create an atmosphere in local government in which the public trust is
upheld. As discussed earlier, codes can help to provide certainty, accountability,
and identity for public officials. At their best, codes can be powerful tools for
improving the ethical climate of local government. But there are also dangers in
overemphasizing the code approach to ethical decision making.

First and most importantly, adopting a code of ethics may take away the
incentive to think critically about one's behavior. There may be a tendency simply to obey the letter of the law (the code) without understanding or considering the underlying rationale for the code's provisions. At worst, one may become like the police officer who, when confronted with the fact that he had lied
about a matter, responded that lying was not specifically prohibited by his
department's code of ethics.[15]

Second, a code that attempts to anticipate and deal with every sort of situation that a public official may confront will be so long and detailed that many
public officials will be unable to understand and follow it. And if a code is not
obeyed by the officials whom it covers, cynicism will likely develop among citizens and among the public officials themselves. To put it in today's jargon, if
one is going to "talk the talk," one also has to "walk the walk." Having no written code of ethics at all is probably better for public confidence than having a
code that is not understood or obeyed.

On the other hand, a code that is short enough to be workable will likely be
quite general and provide few specific answers. It will probably require that
officials weigh situations and make their own judgments. But if a workable code
must be general enough to require an exercise of judgment, perhaps the emphasis of local governments should be on helping public officials learn how to
think critically when ethical dilemmas arise. Such critical thinking will likely involve both the deductive top-down approach and the inductive bottom-out approach described in Chapter 1.

In short, development of skills in ethical decision making is probably far
more important in maintaining public trust than memorizing a detailed set of
pre-ordained behavioral rules or passing more laws. The public trust can only
be preserved if public officials take their calling seriously and make informed
decisions that reflect the core ethical principles that they and their citizens
share.

Questions for Reflection and Application

For Reflection

1. Is adoption of a code of ethics a good idea for a local government? Why or why not?

2. If you prepared a code of ethics, what would it be like? Consider the following issues:

   - *Detail.* How detailed should a code of ethics be? Should it be a complex, legalistic document, a list of general aspirations, or something in-between?
   - *Subjects.* What subjects should a code of ethics cover? Should it deal only with conflicts of interest?
   - *Tone.* Should a code be positive or negative in tone? Is its main purpose to describe standards of conduct to which public officials aspire or to list behavior that is prohibited?
   - *Preparation and Coverage.* Who should prepare a local government's code of ethics? Whom should it cover?

For Application

THE MISSION STATEMENT

A few years ago, Thornton, Colorado, a city of 55,000 located in the Denver Metropolitan Area, tried to develop a community vision to get from where they were to where they wanted to be.[16] City officials used a series of focus group meetings to learn how citizens viewed their city and the surrounding area and what they expected from local government. The city manager then developed and presented to the council the following new mission statement and revised operating philosophy for the city government. The statement and philosophy are in many ways similar to an aspirational code of ethics.

Mission statement. "Our mission is to serve as a catalyst to create a self-sufficient community. Thornton will be responsive to the physical and human requirements of its citizens through innovative leadership and planning. We will ensure the availability of a broad range of services using all available public and private resources."

Operating philosophy. "We are committed to quality leadership for the benefit of our citizens. We will

- Be professional in our attitude and proficient in our tasks;

- Encourage a spirit of cooperation in dealing with the mutual problems and challenges facing our community;
- Expect and demonstrate courtesy and respect in all interactions;
- Commit to excellence in all services provided to our community;
- Be accountable and effective stewards of the public trust and resources;
- Display innovation and initiative in responding to the needs of the community;
- Participate in and promote the exchange of ideas through open communication;
- Recognize that all individuals living and working in the community are essential resources for achieving the City's mission and goals."

Preparation of written statements about where the city was headed was, of course, only a first step. The council and staff intended to work together with their citizens to "get there" through a governance process that emphasized teamwork in setting and achieving goals.

What do you think of Thornton's mission statement and operating philosophy? What are its strengths? What are its weaknesses?

THE "BORROWED" PAPER

[*Based on the case study of "the missing tube" in Mark Pastin,* The Hard Problems of Management: Gaining the Ethics Edge (*San Francisco: Jossey-Bass Inc., Publishers, 1986*), *47–49.*]

The board of commissioners of Truth County has adopted a strict and comprehensive code of conduct for itself, the county manager, county employees under the board's or manager's control, and members of various appointed boards. The code prohibits county employees and officials from having direct or remote financial interests in county business. Those covered by the code are required to refrain from participating in any decisions in which there might be even an appearance of impropriety. The code provides that county officials are to obey both the letter and the spirit of all local, state, and federal laws, and it specifies that any serious violation of its provisions by a county employee is grounds for dismissal. All those covered by the code are to report any violations of the code that they observe.

Soon after the code's adoption, Sue Smart, an employee of the county's finance department, observed her boss, Fred Fraction, a long-time county employee with over twenty-nine years of experience, loading a ten-ream box of typing paper in his car in the county parking lot.

Jokingly, she remarked, "You must have a lot of work to do at home this weekend."

"Oh, this," he replied. "Actually, I need some paper for a civic club project. I reckon I've given this place ten reams worth of free labor and supplies over the last twenty-nine years."

Sue is very troubled by Fred's comment. As noted above, the code specifies that any serious violation of its provisions by a county employee is grounds for dismissal, and there is no question in Sue's mind that theft of county property is a serious violation.

Should Sue report Fred's behavior to the county manager?

Assume that Sue tells the manager. Fred has an outstanding record of service with the county, and he is scheduled to retire next year. At the same time, the manager and the board of commissioners are very concerned about treating everyone the same and making everyone toe the line under the new code.

What should the manager do?

Notes

1. See also the discussion of similar ideas in Terry Cooper, *The Responsible Administrator—An Approach to Ethics for the Administrative Role*, 3d ed. (San Francisco: Jossey-Bass Inc., Publishers, 1990), 141–44.

2. As was pointed out in Chapter 1, this emphasis on differences is somewhat misguided, since we probably do agree for the most part on a number of fundamental principles.

3. John A. Rohr, *Ethics for Bureaucrats: An Essay on Law and Values*, 2d ed. (New York: Marcel Dekker, Inc., 1989), includes an explanation of this approach on pages 68–85 and in several succeeding chapters that show how it works. Perhaps it is our regard for using constitutional principles as ethical norms that explains our interest in United States Supreme Court opinions on constitutional topics such as free speech or reasonable searches and seizures.

4. *See generally* Philip K. Howard, *The Death of Common Sense: How Law Is Suffocating America* (New York: Random House, 1994).

5. *See, e.g.,* Raynor v. Commissioners for the Town of Louisburg, 220 N.C. 348, 352, 17 S.E.2d 495, 498 (1941) (town board's factual determination that an "emergency" exists under North Carolina's competitive bidding statutes is subject to judicial review).

6. Cooper, *The Responsible Administrator,* 124–26. Chapter 5 of Cooper's book discusses the two approaches in detail.

7. *Id.* at 154.

8. Materials from Michael Josephson, "Sample Codes and Policies" in *Ethics Corps: A Training Program on Teaching Ethics in the 90s,* held Nov. 29–Dec. 2, 1993, Airlie, Va. (Marina del Rey, Calif.: Joseph and Edna Josephson Institute for the Advancement of Ethics, 1993), 3–5.

9. *See* N.C. Gen. Stat. § 153A-94 and N.C. Gen. Stat. § 160A-164 (hereinafter the North Carolina General Statutes will be cited as G.S.).

10. Atkins v. City of Charlotte, 296 F. Supp. 1068 (W.D.N.C. 1969) (city could not constitutionally prohibit union membership by municipal employees); Berger v. Battaglia, 779 F.2d 992 (4th Cir. 1985), *cert. denied,* 476 U.S. 1159 (1986) (city could not constitutionally prohibit a particular off-duty entertainment activity by police officer). *See generally* Stephen Allred, *A Legal Guide to Public Employee Free Speech in North Carolina,* 2d ed. (Chapel Hill, N.C.: Institute of Government, The University of North Carolina at Chapel Hill, 1995).

11. For North Carolina cities and counties, for example, this authority is probably inherent in the broad grants of power to create, change, abolish, and consolidate offices, positions, departments, boards, and so forth, and to organize and reorganize city or county government, found in G.S. 160A-146 and 153A-76, respectively.

12. Most local governments that own property can adopt rules that apply to use of that property, even if they do not have the general authority to adopt ordinances, often called the police power.

13. *See, e.g.,* G.S. 160A-174 and G.S. 153A-121, which give such power to North Carolina cities and counties, respectively. In addition local boards of health and local sanitary district boards in North Carolina may adopt rules necessary to protect and promote the public health. *See* G.S. 130A-39(a) and G.S. 130A-55(16), respectively.

14. See, for example, the preemption rules set out in G.S. 160A-174(b) for North Carolina municipalities. The same rules also apply to North Carolina counties.

15. Incident reported by a participant in an ethics session of the Law Enforcement Executives Training Program, held on February 8, 1995, at the Institute of Government.

16. Case reported in Carl H. Neu, Jr., and Jack Ethredge, "Community-Sensible Governance: The Emerging Political Reality of the 21st Century," *National Civic Review* 80 (Fall 1991): 383–85.

Appendix

Appendix

Sample Codes of Ethics

1. International Institute of Municipal Clerks' Professional, Personal Code of Ethics   49

2. Draft Code of Ethics of the North Carolina Association of County Commissioners   51

3. Resolution of Intent of the City Council of the City of Washington [N.C.] Regarding Standards of Conduct for City Officials   57

4. Code of Ethics for Triangle Transit Authority [N.C.] Board of Trustees   61

5. City of Hickory, North Carolina, Documents   67
   Conflict of Interest   67
   Disclosure of Interests Statement [and Certification]   71
   Memorandum [Concerning Approval of Outside Employment]   75
   Request for Approval of Outside Employment   77
   Personnel Ordinance [Excerpts from Article VI. Conflict of Interest and Political Activity]   79

6. International City/County Management Association (ICMA) Code of Ethics with Guidelines   81

7. ICMA Code of Ethics: Rules of Procedure for Enforcement   87

8. Code of Ethics for [N.C.] School Board Members   95

International Institute of Municipal Clerks' Professional, Personal Code of Ethics

Believing in Freedom throughout the World allowing increased cooperation between municipal clerks and other officials, locally, nationally and internationally, I do hereby subscribe to the following principles and ethics which I affirm will govern my personal conduct as municipal clerk:

To uphold constitutional government and the laws of my community;

To so conduct my public and private life as to be an example to my fellow-citizens;

To impart to my profession those standards of quality and integrity that the conduct of the affairs of my office shall be above reproach and to merit public confidence in our community;

To be ever mindful of my neutrality and impartiality, rendering equal service to all and to extend the same treatment I wish to receive myself;

To record that which is true and preserve that which is entrusted to me as if it were my own; and

To strive constantly to improve the administration of the affairs of my office consistent with applicable laws and through sound management practices to produce continued progress and so fulfill my responsibilities to my community and others.

These things, I, as municipal clerk, do pledge to do in the interest and purposes for which our government has been established.

_____
Signature

Source: International Institute of Municipal Clerks. Reprinted with permission.

Draft Code of Ethics of the North Carolina Association of County Commissioners

Preamble

The stability and proper operation of democratic representative government depends upon the continuing consent of the governed, upon the public confidence in the integrity of the government and upon responsible exercise of the trust conferred by the people. Government decisions and policy must be made and implemented through proper channels and processes of the governmental structure. The purpose of this code is to establish guidelines for ethical standards of conduct for county commissioners. It should not be considered a substitute for the law or a county commissioner's best judgment.

County commissioners must be able to act in a manner to maintain their integrity and independence, yet must be responsive to the interests and needs of those they represent. County commissioners serve in an important advocacy capacity in meeting the needs of their citizens and should recognize the legitimacy of this role as well as the intrinsic importance of this function to the proper functioning of representative government. At the same time, county commissioners must, at times, act in an adjudicatory or administrative capacity and must, when doing so, act in a fair and impartial manner. County commissioners must know how to distinguish these roles and when each role is appropriate and they must act accordingly. County commissioners must be aware of their obligation to conform their behavior to standards of ethical conduct that warrant the trust of their constituents. Each county commissioner must find within his or her own conscience the touchstone on which to determine appropriate conduct.

Canon One

A County Commissioner Shall Obey the Law

County commissioners shall support the Constitution of the United States, the Constitution of North Carolina and the laws enacted by the Congress of the United States and the General Assembly pursuant thereto.

Canon Two

A County Commissioner Should Uphold the Integrity and Independence of His or Her Office

County Commissioners should demonstrate the highest standards of personal integrity, truthfulness, honesty and fortitude in all their public activities in order to inspire public confidence and trust in county government. County commissioners should participate in establishing, maintaining, and enforcing, and should themselves observe, high standards of conduct so that the integrity and independence of their office may be preserved. The provisions of this Code should be construed and applied to further these objectives.

Canon Three

A County Commissioner Should Avoid Impropriety and the Appearance of Impropriety in All His or Her Activities

A. It is essential that county government attract those citizens best qualified and willing to serve. County commissioners have legitimate interests—economic, professional and vocational—of a private nature. County commissioners should not be denied, and should not deny to other county commissioners or citizens, the opportunity to acquire, retain and pursue private interests, economic or otherwise, except when conflicts with their responsibility to the public cannot be avoided. County commissioners must exercise their best judgment to determine when this is the case.

B. County commissioners should respect and comply with the law and should conduct themselves at all times in a manner that promotes public confidence in the integrity of the office of county commissioner and of county government.

C. County commissioners should not allow family, social, or other relationships to unduly influence their conduct or judgment and should not lend the prestige of the office of county commissioner to advance the private interests of others; nor should they convey or permit others to convey the impression that they are in a special position to influence them.

Canon Four

A County Commissioner Should Perform the Duties of the Office Diligently

County commissioners should, while performing the duties of the office as prescribed by law, give precedence to these duties over other activities. In the performance of these duties, the following standards should apply:

A. Legislative Responsibilities

1. County commissioners should actively pursue policy goals they believe to be in the best interests of their constituents within the parameters of orderly decision-making, rules of the Board of County Commissioners and open government.

2. County commissioners should respect the legitimacy of the goals and interests of other county commissioners and should respect the rights of others to pursue goals and policies different from their own.

B. Adjudicative Responsibilities

1. County commissioners should be faithful to the general and local laws pertaining to the office and strive for professional competence in them. They should be unswayed by partisan interests, public clamor, or fear of criticism.

2. County commissioners should demand and contribute to the maintenance of order and decorum in proceedings before the Board of County Commissioners.

3. County commissioners should be honest, patient, dignified and courteous to those with whom they deal in their official capacity, and should require similar conduct of their staff and others subject to their direction and control.

4. County commissioners should accord to every person who is legally interested in a proceeding before the commission full right to be heard according to law.

5. County commissioners should dispose promptly of the business of the county for which they are responsible.

C. Administrative Responsibilities

1. County commissioners should clearly distinguish legislative, adjudicatory and administrative responsibilities and should refrain from inappropriate interference in the impartial administration of county affairs by county employees. Commissioners should diligently discharge those administrative responsibilities that are appropriate, should maintain professional competence in the administration of these duties and should facilitate the diligent discharge of the administrative responsibilities of fellow commissioners and other county officials.

2. County commissioners should conserve the resources of the county in their charge. They should employ county equipment, property, funds and personnel only in legally permissible pursuits and in a manner that exemplifies excellent stewardship.

3. County commissioners should require county employees subject to their direction and control to observe the standards of fidelity and diligence that apply to commissioners as well as those appropriate for employees.

4. County commissioners should take or initiate appropriate disciplinary measures against a county employee for improper conduct of which the commissioner may become aware.

5. County commissioners should not employ or recommend the appointment of unnecessary employees and should exercise the power of employment only on the basis of merit, avoid favoritism and refrain from illegal discrimination and nepotism. They should not approve compensation of employees beyond the fair value of services rendered.

Canon Five

A County Commissioner Should Conduct the Affairs of the Board in an Open and Public Manner

County commissioners should be aware of the letter and intent of the State's Open Meetings Law, should conduct the affairs of the Board of County Commissioners consistent with the letter and spirit of that law and consistent with the need to inspire and maintain public confidence in the integrity and fairness of county government and the office of county commissioner. Consistent with this goal of preserving public trust, county commissioners should be aware of the need for discretion in deliberations when the lack of discretion would pose a threat to the resources of the county, to the reputation of current or potential county employees, to orderly and responsible decision making, to the integrity of other governmental processes or to other legitimate interests of the county.

Canon Six

A County Commissioner Should Regulate His or Her Extra-Governmental Activities to Minimize the Risk of Conflict with His or Her Official Duties

A. County commissioners should inform themselves concerning campaign finance, conflict of interest and other appropriate state and federal laws and should scrupulously comply with the provisions of such laws.
B. County commissioners should refrain from financial and business dealings that tend to reflect adversely on the Board or on county government or to interfere with the proper performance of official duties.
C. County commissioners should manage their personal financial interests to minimize the number of cases in which they must abstain from voting on matters coming before the Board.
D. Information acquired by county commissioners in their official capacity should not be used or disclosed in financial dealings or for any other purpose not related to official duties.

Canon Seven

A County Commissioner Should Refrain from Political Activity Inappropriate to His or Her Office

A. County commissioners have a civic responsibility to support good government by every available means, to continue to inform and educate the citizenry about the affairs and processes of county government, and to make themselves available to citizens of the county so that they may ascertain and respond to the needs of the community. In doing so, county commissioners may and should join or affiliate with civic organizations whether partisan or non-partisan, may and should attend political meetings, may and should advocate and support the principles or policies of civic or political organizations consistent with the Constitution and laws of the United States and North Carolina.
B. Candidates for the office of county commissioner, including incumbents:
   1. Should inform themselves concerning the laws of this state with regard to campaigns and relevant disclosure requirements and should scrupulously comply with the provisions of such laws;
   2. Should maintain the dignity appropriate to the office, and should encourage members of their families to adhere to the same standards of political conduct that apply to commissioners;

3. Should not make pledges or promises of conduct in office that they will not or cannot perform or would be illegal if it were performed;
4. Should not misrepresent their identity, qualifications, present position, or other fact; and
5. Should avoid pledges or promises of conduct in office other than the faithful and impartial performance of the duties of the office.

Source: Handout from session on "Ethics" at 1991 Conference of the North Carolina Association of County Commissioners. Prepared by James B. Blackburn, III, Association General Counsel. Reprinted with permission.

Resolution of Intent of the City Council of the City of Washington [N.C.] Regarding Standards of Conduct for City Officials

WHEREAS, the proper operation of democratic government requires that public officials and employees be independent, impartial and responsible to the people; and

WHEREAS, government decisions and policy must be made in proper channels of the governmental structure; and

WHEREAS, the public office must not be used for personal gain; and

WHEREAS, the public must have confidence in the integrity of its government.

In recognition of these goals, BE IT RESOLVED BY THE CITY COUNCIL OF THE CITY OF WASHINGTON, as follows:

1. That this resolution of intent be adopted to establish guidelines for ethical standards of conduct for all such officials by setting forth some of those acts or actions that may be incompatible with the best interest of the City of Washington. To that end, all city officials, hereinafter defined as including the Mayor, members of the City Council, City Manager, Department Heads, the City Attorney and all other City employees shall be subject to and abide by the following standards of conduct:

   (a) No city official shall have or hereafter acquire an interest in any contract or agreement with the City if he will privately benefit or profit from the contracting or undertaking in violation of North Carolina General Statutes 14-234.

   (b) No city official shall use his official position on the City's facilities for his private gain, nor shall he appear before or represent any private person, group or interest before any department, agency, commission or board of the City except in matters of purely civic or public concern. The provisions of this paragraph are not intended to prohibit city official's use of parking permits and are not intended to prohibit his speaking before neighborhood groups and other non-profit organizations.

(c) No city official shall use or disclose confidential information gained in the course of or by reason of his official position for purposes of advancing his financial or personal interest.

(d) No city official shall engage in, or accept private employment or render service, for private interest when such employment or service is incompatible with the proper discharge of his official duties or would tend to impair his independence of judgment or action in the performance of his official duties, unless otherwise permitted by law.

(e) No city official shall directly or indirectly solicit any gift; or accept or receive any gift having a value of Fifty Dollars ($50.00) or more, whether in the form of money, services, loan, travel, entertainment, hospitality, thing or promise, or any other form, under circumstances in which it could reasonably be inferred that the gift was intended to influence him, or could reasonably be expected to influence as a reward for any official action on his part. Legitimate political contributions shall not be considered as gifts under the provisions of this paragraph.

(f) No city official shall grant any special consideration, treatment or advantage to any citizen beyond that which is available to every other citizen.

2. BE IT FURTHER RESOLVED that this resolution of intent shall be subject to enforcement in the following manner, said sanctions being the exclusive remedies available hereunder.

(a) The City Manager shall take whatever lawful disciplinary action he deems appropriate, including but not limited to, reprimand, suspension, demotion or termination of service, for any officer, department head or employee in the administrative service of the City under his jurisdiction who he finds has violated this resolution of intent.

(b) For all other persons, the City Council may adopt a resolution of censure which shall be placed as a matter of record in the minutes of an official Council meeting.

(c) No sanction provided for hereunder shall be invoked until an adequate investigation shall have been made and the person charged with the violation shall have been afforded all of his legal and constitutional rights including a due process hearing, the right to present evidence, to cross-examine the witnesses and to be represented by counsel at the hearing, upon the request of the person so charged.

3. BE IT FURTHER RESOLVED that copies of the foregoing resolution be distributed to all public officials effected hereunder, present and future; and that the City Manager and the City Attorney for the City of Washington be instructed to periodically on at least an annual basis present an instructional program for the benefit of the persons effected by this resolution informing them of its implications.

DULY ADOPTED THIS 8th day of October, 1990.

Sam Fowle
MAYOR

ATTEST:

CITY CLERK: Rita A. Thompson

Source: City of Washington, N.C. Reprinted with permission.

Code of Ethics for Triangle Transit Authority [N.C.] Board of Trustees

Section 1. Declaration of Policy

(a) The proper operation of democratic government requires that public officials and employees be independent, impartial and responsible to the people; that governmental decisions and policy be made publicly; that public office not be used for personal gain; and that the public maintain confidence in the integrity of its government.

(b) In recognition of these goals, a code of ethics for Authority officials is hereby adopted. The purpose of this article is to set forth guidelines for ethical standards of conduct for all such officials by setting forth acts or actions that are incompatible with the best interests of the Authority.

Section 2. Definitions

As used in this article, the following terms shall have the meaning indicated:

Business entity means any business, proprietorship, firm, partnership, person in representative or fiduciary capacity, association, venture, trust or corporation which is organized for financial gain or profit;

Authority official means the General Manager, members of the Authority Board of Trustees (including ex officio members), department heads, and any employees involved in purchasing or acquiring goods and services.

Immediate family means the Authority official, his/her spouse, children (including stepchildren and foster children), brothers, sisters, mother, father, mother-in-law, father-in-law, sisters-in-law, and brothers-in-law.

Close business associate means an individual who is directly engaged in business with the authority official through partnership or ownership in which either the Authority Official or an immediate family member and the close business associate each control or own in excess of five (5) percent of the stock in a business entity.

Interest means direct or indirect pecuniary or material benefit, as a result of an official act, a contract, or transaction with the Authority, accruing to:

(1) An Authority Official;

(2) Any person in his/her immediate family;

(3) Any business entity in which the Authority Official, member of his/her immediate family, or a close business associate is, or is about to be, an officer or director.

(4) Any business entity in which in excess of five (5) percent of the stock, or legal or beneficial ownership of, is controlled or owned directly or indirectly by the Authority Official, his/her immediate family member, or close business associate.

(5) An organization which employs or is about to employ the Authority Official, his/her immediate family member, or close business associate.

For the purposes of the above paragraphs 2, 3, 4, and 5, an Authority Official is presumed to have knowledge of the financial affairs of his/her spouse and minor children. For the purpose of this policy, the Authority Official only has an interest in the affairs of other immediate family members or close business associates if the Authority Official has knowledge of or should have known of the interest of the family members or close business associate.

Official act or action means any legislative, administrative, appointive, or discretionary act of any Authority Official.

Confidential information means any information or knowledge which has not been made public through the regular affairs of government. Information that has become public knowledge, whether or not through the regular affairs of government, is not considered confidential information.

Section 3. Standards of Conduct

All Authority Officials as defined in this article shall be subject to and abide by the following standards of conduct.

(a) *Interest in contract or agreement.* No Authority Official shall participate in selection or award of a contract if a conflict of interest, real or apparent, would be involved (as determined by the Board of Trustees pursuant to Section 4). Such a conflict would arise when: an Authority Official, Authority Official's immediate family member, Authority Official's close business associate or an organization which employs, or is about to employ any of the above, has an interest in the firm about to be selected for an award.

(b) *Use of official position.* No Authority Official shall use his/her official position or the Authority's facilities for his/her private gain. No Authority Official shall appear before or represent any private person, group or interest before any department, committee, or Board of the Authority except in matters of purely civil or public concern. The provisions of this paragraph are not intended to prohibit an Authority Official from speaking before neighborhood groups and other nonprofit organizations.

(c) *Disclosure of information.* No Authority Official shall use or disclose confidential information gained in the course of or by reason of his/her official position with the Authority for purposes of advancing:

(1) His/her financial or personal interest;

(2) The interest of a business entity of which the Authority Official, an immediate family member, or close business associate has an interest; or,

(3) The financial or personal interest of a member of his/her immediate family or that of a close business associate;

(4) The financial or personal interest of any citizen beyond that which is available to every other citizen.

(d) *Incompatible service.* No Authority Official shall engage in, or accept private employment or render service for private interest, when such employment or service is incompatible with the proper discharge of his/her official duties with the Authority or would tend to impair his/her independence of judgment or action in the performance of his/her official duties with the Authority, unless otherwise permitted by law and unless disclosure is made as provided in this article.

(e) *Gifts.* No Authority Official shall directly or indirectly solicit any gift, or accept or receive any gift, whether in the form of money, services, loan, travel, entertainment, hospitality, thing or promise, or any other form, under circumstances in which a reasonable person would believe that the gift was intended to influence him/her in the performance of his/her official duties, or was intended as a reward for any official action on his/her part. Legitimate political contributions to Authority Officials shall not be considered as gifts under the provisions of this paragraph. North Carolina General Statute 133-32 provides additional guidance concerning gifts and favors.

Exempted from the prohibition are reasonable honorariums for participating in meetings, advertising items or souvenirs of nominal value or meals furnished at banquets. Also exempted are customary gifts or favors between

Authority Officials or officers and their friends or relatives. Authority Officials must report in writing to the Secretary of the Authority honorariums and gifts and favors from friends and relatives if made by a covered contractor, subcontractor, or supplier.

(f) *Special Treatment.* No Authority Official shall grant any special consideration, treatment, or advantage to any citizen beyond that which is available to every other citizen.

Section 4. Disclosure of Interest in Legislative Action

Officers of the Triangle Transit Authority or any member of the Board of Trustees who have an interest in any business before the Board shall publicly disclose on the record of the Board the nature and extent of such interest, and shall withdraw from any consideration of the matter if excused by the Board. It is a violation of this policy for an Authority official who has an interest in some business before the Authority to advocate, whether publicly or privately, that interest to other Authority officials.

Section 5. General Disclosure

(a) All Authority officials, as herein defined, shall file with the General Manager on the first day of February of each year, a statement containing the following information:

(1) The identity by name and address, of any business entity of which the Authority Official, his/her spouse, or his/her minor children is an owner (as defined in section 2 of this chapter), official or director. Additionally, the Authority Official and spouse shall give the name of their employer or, if self-employed, state the nature of their work.

(2) The identity, by location and address, of all real property located in the three-county area owned by the Authority Official, his/her spouse, or his/her minor children, including an option to purchase or lease.

(b) The statements required by this section shall be filed on a form prescribed by the General Manager and are public records available for inspection and copying by any person during normal business hours. The General Manager is authorized to establish and charge reasonable fees for the copying of these statements.

Section 6. Investigations Instigated by the Board of Trustees, General Manager, Any Other Person

(a) The Board of Trustees may direct the Authority Attorney to investigate any apparent violation of this article, as it applies to the Chair of the Board of Trustees, any member of the Board of Trustees, or the General Manager, and to report the finding of his/her investigation to the Board of Trustees.

(b) The General Manager may investigate any apparent violation of this article as it applies to Authority employees covered by this ethics policy.

(c) The Board of Trustees may direct the General Manager to investigate any apparent violation of this article by the Authority Attorney and to report the findings of his/her investigation to the Board of Trustees.

(d) Any person who believes that a violation of this article has occurred may file a complaint in writing with the Board of Trustees when the Chair of the Board, a member of the Board, or the General Manager is the subject of the complaint, or with the General Manager when an employee is the subject of the complaint, who may thereafter proceed as provided by paragraphs a, b, and c of this section.

Section 7. Sanctions by the General Manager, Board of Trustees; Rights of Accused at Hearings

(a) If the General Manager, after the receipt of an investigation, has cause to believe a violation of this article has occurred, he/she shall take whatever lawful disciplinary action he/she deems appropriate, including but not limited to, reprimand, suspension, demotion, or termination of service.

(b) If the Board of Trustees, after receipt of an investigation from the Authority Attorney, has cause to believe a violation has occurred, the Board of Trustees shall schedule a hearing on this matter. The official who is charged with the violation shall have the right to present evidence, cross-examine witnesses, including the complainant or complainants, and be represented by counsel at the hearing. If, after such hearing and review of all the evidence, the Board of Trustees, by official action as defined by Article II, Section 7 of the Authority's bylaws, finds a violation has occurred, the Board may adopt a resolution of censure which shall be placed as a matter of record in the minutes of an official Board meeting, and shall be immediately communicated to the Board member's appointing body.

Section 8. Advisory Opinions

When any Authority Official has a doubt as to the applicability of any provision of this article to a particular situation involving that Authority Official, or as to the definition of terms used in this article, he/she may apply to the Authority Attorney for an advisory opinion. The Authority Official shall have the opportunity to present the Authority Official's interpretation of the facts at issue and of the applicability of provisions of this article before such advisory opinion is made.

Source: Triangle Transit Authority, Research Triangle Park, N.C. Reprinted with permission.

City of Hickory, North Carolina, Documents

Conflict of Interest

(To be made a part of the Personnel Ordinance near the Ordinance
Governing Political Activity of Employees)

Conflicts Resulting in Financial Gain

A. Definitions

For purposes of this section, the following definitions shall apply:

1. *Business Entity* means any business, proprietorship, firm, partnership, person in representative or fiduciary capacity, association, venture, trust or corporation which is organized for financial gain or for profit.

2. *City Official* means the Mayor, members of the City Council, City Manager, Assistant City Manager, City Attorney, and Department Heads.

3. *Immediate Household* means the City Official, his/her spouse, and all dependent children of the City Official.

4. *Interest* means direct or indirect pecuniary or material benefit accruing to a City Official as a result of a contract or transaction which is or may be the subject of an official act or action by or with the City. For purposes of this article, a City Official shall be deemed to have an interest in the affairs of (1) any person in his immediate household as such term is defined in this section, (2) any business entity in which the City Official is an officer or director, (3) any business entity in which an excess of five percent (5%) of the stock of or legal or beneficial ownership of is controlled or owned directly or indirectly by the City Official, (4) any non-profit organization on which the Mayor or any member of the City Council currently serves as an officer, director, or board member.

5. *Official act or action* means any legislative, administrative, appointive, or discretionary act of any City Official.

B. Standards of Conduct

1. *Scope.* All City Officials as defined in this article shall be subject to and abide by the following standards of conduct.

2. *Interest in Contract or Agreement.* No City Official herein defined shall have or thereafter acquire an interest in any contract or agreement with the

City. This section does not prevent employment contracts between the City Official and the City.

3. *Use of Official Position.* No City Official shall use his or her official position or the City's facilities for his or her private gain. In addition, City Officials shall not misuse their status in such a way as to require, expect, or accept favors from subordinate employees.

4. *Disclosure of Information.* No City Official shall use or disclose confidential information gained in the course of or by reason of his official position for purposes of advancing (1) his or her financial or personal interest, (2) a business entity in which he or she is an owner in part or in whole, an officer or director, (3) the financial or personal interest of a member of his or her immediate household or that of any other person.

5. *Incompatible Service.* No City Official shall engage in or accept private employment or render service to private or other public interests when such employment or service is incompatible with the proper discharge of official duties or would tend to impair independence of judgment or action in the performance of official duties unless otherwise permitted by law and unless disclosure is made as provided in this article. Before accepting private employment, the City Official should consider whether such employment would impact the City negatively. A City Official who accepts private employment should not represent himself or herself as an employee or agent of the City of Hickory.

6. *Gifts.* No City Official shall directly or indirectly solicit any gift or accept or receive any gift having a value of Twenty-Five Dollars ($25.00) or more whether in the form of money, services loaned, travel, entertainment, hospitality, thing or promise or any other form under circumstances in which it could reasonably be inferred that the gift was intended to influence him or her or could reasonably be expected to influence him or her in the performance of official duties or is intended as a reward for any official action on his or her part. Legitimate political contributions shall not be considered as gifts under the provisions of this paragraph.

7. *Special Treatment.* No City Official shall grant any special consideration, treatment, or advantage to any citizen or public or private entity beyond that which is available to every other citizen or entity.

C. Disclosure of Interest in Legislative Action

The Mayor or any member of the City Council who has an interest in the official act or action before the Council shall publicly disclose on the record of the Council the nature and extent of such interest and shall withdraw from any consideration of the matter if excused by the Council pursuant to City Charter.

D. General Disclosure—City Clerk to Prescribe Form and Fees
   1. All City Officials as herein defined shall file with the City Clerk on the 1st day of July 1992 a statement containing the following information: (1) The identity by name and address of any business entity of which he or she or any member of his or her immediate household is an owner, officer or director and percentage of interest or ownership, if applicable. Additionally, the City Official and spouse shall give the name of their employer or if self-employed, state the nature of their work. (2) The identity by location and address of all real property located in the Hickory Regional Planning Area owned by the City Official or any member of his or her immediate household, including an option to purchase or lease for ten years or more other than personal residence. (3) The identity by name and address of any non-profit organization which was the subject of some official act or action of the City within the past year and on which the City Official or spouse serves as an officer, director or board member. In addition, the City Official should provide names of other board members of any entity on which the City Official serves.
   2. The statements required by this section shall be filed on a form prescribed by the City Clerk and are public records available for inspection and copying by any person during normal business hours. The City Clerk shall charge the City's prescribed fee for the copying of statements. City Officials are responsible for updating this disclosure statement any time there is any change in the City Official's ownership or status as defined by this section.

E. Investigations Instigated by City Council, City Manager or Any Other Person
   1. City Council may direct the City Attorney to investigate any apparent violation of this article as it applies to the Mayor, any member of the City Council, or City Manager, and to report the findings of the investigation to the City Council.
   2. The City Manager may direct the Staff Attorney to investigate any apparent violation of this article as it applies to the Assistant City Manager and Department Heads and to report the findings of the investigation to the City Manager.
   3. The City Council may direct the City Manager to investigate any apparent violation of this article by the City Attorney and to report the findings of the investigation to the City Council.
   4. Any person who believes that a violation of this article has occurred may file a complaint in writing with the City Council when the Mayor and members of the City Council, City Manager, or City Attorney are the subjects of the complaint, or with the City Manager when the Assistant City Manager or Department Heads are the subjects of the complaint

and may thereafter proceed as provided in paragraph one through three of this section.

F. Sanctions by City Manager and City Council, Rights of Accused at Hearings
   1. If the City Manager, after receipt of an investigation, has cause to believe a violation has occurred, a hearing shall be scheduled on the matter. The hearing shall be conducted in accordance with Personnel provisions of the North Carolina General Statutes and City Charter. The City Official who is charged with the violation shall have the right to present evidence, cross-examine witnesses, including the complainant or complainants, and be represented by counsel at the hearing. If after such hearing and a review of all the evidence the City Manager finds that a violation of this article has occurred, he shall take whatever lawful disciplinary action he deems appropriate, including but not limited to reprimand, suspension, demotion, or termination.
   2. If the City Council, after receipt of an investigation, has cause to believe a violation has occurred, the City Council shall schedule a hearing on the matter, said hearing may be held as an Executive Session. The City Official who is charged with the violation shall have the right to present evidence, cross-examine witnesses, including the complainant or complainants, and be represented by counsel at the hearing. If upon the conclusion of the hearing, the majority vote of the Council finds a violation has occurred, the Council may adopt a resolution of censure which shall be placed as a matter of record in the minutes of an official Council meeting.

G. Advisory Opinions
   When a City Official has a doubt as to the applicability of any provision of this article to a particular situation or to the definition of terms used in this article, he may apply to the City or Staff Attorney for an advisory opinion, either of which shall issue an opinion in writing and file same with either the City Council or City Attorney. The City Official shall have the opportunity to present his or her interpretation of the facts at issue and of the application of provisions of this article before such advisory opinion is made. In addition, the City Official shall publicly disclose to the City Council or City Manager the facts of issue in a particular situation and shall rely upon any resolution adopted by the City Council or City Manager regarding that particular situation.

Source: City of Hickory, N.C. Reprinted with permission.

Disclosure of Interests Statement

(To Be Filed in City Clerk's Office on or before July 1, 1992)

1. Your Name: _____

   Your Address: _____

   Your Employer: _____

   Nature of Work: _____

2. Names of other adult persons in your immediate household and their employer(s). If self-employed, state the nature of work:

Name	Employer	Nature of Work

3.A. List the name and address of any *business entity* in which you or any member of your immediate household is an owner, officer, or director and state the percentage of interest or ownership, if applicable:

Entity	Address	% Interest/ Ownership	Person(s) Having This Interest

   B. For each entity listed above, state the names and addresses of other officers and directors.

Entity	Officers/Directors and Addresses

4.A. State the names and addresses of any non-profit organizations in which you or your spouse is an officer, director, or board member:

Organization   Address   Position   By Whom

_____

_____

_____

_____

B. For each organization listed above, state the names and addresses of other officers, directors, or board members:

Organization   Officers/Directors/
                                Board Members and
                                Addresses

_____

_____

_____

_____

5. Identify by location and address all real property located in the Hickory Regional Planning Area owned by you or any member of your immediate household, including any options to purchase or lease for 10 or more years:

Property   Location   Owner

_____

_____

_____

_____

Certification

The above information is an all inclusive account of the business, organizational, and real estate (Hickory Regional Planning Area only) interests by me or any member of my immediate household. I understand that this statement must be filed in the Office of the City Clerk at 76 North Center Street, Hickory, N.C., on or before July of each year. I further understand that this statement constitutes a public record and is available for public inspection.

Date   Signature

_____   _____

STATE OF NORTH CAROLINA
COUNTY OF

I, _____ , Notary Public for county
of _____ and state of North Carolina do hereby
certify that _____ personally appeared before me
this day and acknowledged the due execution of the foregoing instrument.

Witness my hand and official seal this _____ day of _____ , 1992.

_____
Notary Public

SEAL

My commission expires: _____

(Conflict of Interest Ordinance Adopted June 2, 1992, by the City Council of the City of Hickory, N.C., attached hereto.)
Source: City of Hickory. Reprinted with permission.

Memorandum [Concerning Approval of Outside Employment]

DATE: February 10, 1992
TO: Department Heads
FROM: Jack Lindsay, Personnel Director
SUBJECT: Approval of Outside Employment
          (Personnel Ordinance, Article VI, Section 2)

The attached form will help department heads to be uniform in carrying out their responsibility regarding outside employment. Informal, unrecorded approval is adequate for small jobs which have no obvious conflict of interest—that is, two employees helping each other repair a car, even if some payment is made. The department head may delegate the responsibility for approval to the division head or first-line supervisor. Before this responsibility can be delegated, the supervisor must be instructed by the department head in the City's policy regarding outside employment and must know when a written request for approval is required.

The signed request for approval form should be used for any one of these kinds of employment:

a. At any time there is a company paycheck, and the employee is on a company payroll.

b. At any time a City employee is doing private work for any department head, either paid or unpaid.

c. When the work is on a regular basis or involves a contract. A "regular basis" includes work over a period of three days or three partial days within one week, involving more than 16 hours of work within a 7-day period for the same "employer," or more than 40 hours in any 30-day period for the same employer—and is performed repeatedly or on a regular basis.

d. At any time the employee or the department head wishes to avoid the appearance of a conflict of interest.

Employees whose secondary job involves agreements or contracts with numerous individuals are required to fill out only one form each year, unless a particular job falls into one of the four categories above. For example, an employee who moonlights as an auto mechanic on a regular basis will fill out only one form, notifying the City of his/her secondary job and obtaining approval only once. However, at any time the employee repairs a department head's car, then a separate form will be required. Another example, an employee who does yard work during the summer and has regular customers by oral agreements would be required to fill out only one form at the beginning of each season or once a year.

However, if the employee mows the grass for a department head, then a separate form will be required each season (or the original request for approval will state that his/her customers include a department head or department heads).

The Police Department will follow their General Order 84-10 regarding "Off-Duty Employment, Part-Time Jobs, or Secondary Employment," which has been in effect in some form since 1984.

Other department heads may develop their own procedures regarding outside employment, providing they are first approved by the City Manager and on file in the Personnel Department before becoming effective. Any procedures developed must be in agreement with the personnel ordinance requirements for outside employment and with the Conflict of Interest policy for City Officials.

Department heads and division heads should notify applicant finalists that a job with the City must take priority over secondary employment. The Personnel Department will notify new employees of the personnel ordinance requirements on outside employment and the conflict of interest policy at Orientation. Department heads and their supervisory staff will inform their supervisors and current employees of their procedure for obtaining approval of outside employment and will submit all written requests, whether approved or disapproved, to the Personnel Department. A copy will be sent by the Personnel Department to the City Manager.

Source: City of Hickory, N.C. Reprinted with permission.

Request for Approval of Outside Employment

Use of this form will assist in compliance with the Personnel Ordinance, Article VI, Section 2, *Outside Employment*: The work of the City of Hickory shall have precedence over the other occupational interests of employees. All outside employment must be reported to and approved by an employee's department head. Conflicting outside employment shall be grounds for dismissal or other disciplinary action. Article V, Section 20, *Use of City Property and Equipment*: City equipment, materials, tools, and supplies shall not be available for personal use nor be removed from City property, except in the conduct of official City business.

See also the City of Hickory *Conflict of Interest Policy*, a portion of which is printed on the reverse side of this form.

Employee name, printed _____

Department/division _____

Name of "outside" employer:
(Type of work, and company or persons for whom work is being done)
_____
_____

Address or location of outside employer or location of work
_____
_____

Date outside work begins _____

Estimated date the outside work will end _____

   My signature below certifies that I will report to my City supervisor any injuries on my second job and will not attempt to claim worker's compensation from the City of Hickory based on injuries received on another job.

Employee signature _____ Date _____

Restrictions or other comments by department head: _____
_____
_____

Signature (approval) by department head:
_____ Date _____

Send this form after approval or disapproval by the department head to the Personnel Department for the employee's personnel record. A copy will be sent by the Personnel Department to the City Manager.

(Reverse side of form)

Excerpts from the City of Hickory Conflict of Interest Policy

(The entire policy is available from the City Clerk or any Department Head)

Standards of Conduct

Scope: All City Officials . . . shall be subject to and abide by the following standards of conduct.

Interest in Contract or Agreement: No City Official . . . shall have or thereafter acquire an interest in any contract or agreement with the City. This section does not prevent employment contracts between the City Official and the City.

Use of Official Position: No City Official shall use his or her official position or the City's facilities for his or her private gain. In addition, City Officials shall not misuse their status in such a way as to require, expect, or accept favors from subordinate employees.

Disclosure of Information: No City Official shall use or disclose confidential information gained in the course of or by reason of his official position for purposes of advancing (1) his or her financial or personal interest, (2) a business entity in which he or she is an owner in part or in whole, an officer or director, (3) the financial or personal interest of a member of his or her immediate household or that of any other person.

Incompatible Service: No City Official shall engage in or accept private employment or render service to private or other public interests when such employment or service is incompatible with the proper discharge of official duties or would tend to impair independence of judgment or action in the performance of official duties unless otherwise permitted by law and unless disclosure is made as provided in this article. Before accepting private employment, the City Official should consider whether such employment would impact the City negatively. A City Official who accepts private employment should not represent himself or herself as an employee or agent of the City of Hickory.

Gifts: No City Official shall directly or indirectly solicit any gift or accept or receive any gift having a value of Twenty-Five Dollars ($25.00) or more whether in the form of money, services loaned, travel, entertainment, hospitality, thing or promise or any other form under circumstances in which it could reasonably be inferred that the gift was intended to influence him or her or could reasonably be expected to influence him or her in the performance of official duties or is intended as a reward for any official action on his or her part. Legitimate political contributions shall not be considered as gifts under the provisions of this paragraph.

Special Treatment: No City Official shall grant any special consideration, treatment, or advantage to any citizen or public or private entity beyond that which is available to every other citizen or entity.

See the complete policy for additional information regarding (1) disclosure of interest in legislative action, (2) general disclosure on form prescribed by the city clerk, (3) investigations by the City Council, (4) rights of accused, (5) disciplinary action or censure, and (6) advisory opinions from the City Attorney or Staff Attorney regarding interpretation of this policy.

Source: City of Hickory, N.C. Reprinted with permission.

Personnel Ordinance

ARTICLE VI. Conflict of Interest and Political Activity

SECTION 1. *Applicability of Article.* The provisions of this article shall be applicable to all employees except those exempted in Article I, Section 4.

SECTION 2. *Outside Employment.* The work of the governmental unit shall have precedence over the other occupational interests of employees. All outside employment must be reported to and approved by an employee's department head. Conflicting outside employment shall be grounds for dismissal or other disciplinary action.

SECTION 3. *Political Activity.* The city encourages an employee to exercise civic responsibility in supporting good government at all levels by voting for the political candidates and issues of his or her choice.

An employee may join or affiliate with political organizations, may attend political meetings, and may advocate and support political principles and policies in accordance with the constitution and laws of the State of North Carolina and of the United States of America.

However, an employee shall not

(a) Engage in political activity while on duty;
(b) Be required to contribute funds or support for political or partisan purposes as a condition of employment, pay raise, promotion or tenure of office;
(c) Solicit or act as custodian of funds for political or partisan purposes associated with the City of Hickory;
(d) Use city-owned supplies, equipment, or facilities to display political slogans, posters, or stickers or for any other political purpose;
(e) Be a candidate for, or hold political office in the City of Hickory.

Any violation of these provisions shall be deemed improper conduct and may result in discharge or other disciplinary action.

. . . .

SECTION 20. *Use of City Property and Equipment.* City equipment, materials, tools, and supplies shall not be available for personal use nor be removed from city property, except in the conduct of official City business. Regulations governing the use and operation of City equipment shall be prescribed by the City Manager and amended as required.

SECTION 21. *On-the-Job Injury or Illness.* An employee who becomes ill or is injured in the performance of duties shall immediately report the illness or injury to the supervisor. The employee will provide the supervisor with the necessary information to complete required forms or reports as required by the Occupational Safety and Health Act (OSHA). The employee's supervisor or department head shall be responsible for immediately reporting the injury or illness to the Personnel Department.

SECTION 22. *Accidents Involving City Equipment.* Accidents involving injuries of employees, other personnel, or damage to someone else's property occurring while using city equipment or damage to city equipment shall be reported immediately by the employee to his/her supervisor. The supervisor will be responsible for taking appropriate action and notifying his/her superior. The employee's supervisor or department head shall be responsible for immediately reporting the accident to the personnel department.

SECTION 23. *Conditions of Employment.* All employees will be required to comply with safety and health standards, rules, regulations and departmental orders issued in accordance with the Occupational Safety and Health Act (OSHA).

SECTION 24. *City Equipment and Property.*

   A. All employees whose employment with the city has terminated shall be responsible for returning all City of Hickory property and equipment issued to them during their employment. This includes but is not limited to safety equipment, uniforms, parking cards, and all other City property. The terminating employee shall reimburse the City for any damage or loss occurring to the property entrusted to them.

   B. A terminated employee's final payroll check shall be forwarded to the Personnel Department by the Finance Department to be held until all City equipment has been returned or the City has been reimbursed.

May 15, 1990

Source: City of Hickory, N.C. Reprinted with permission.

International City/County Management Association (ICMA) Code of Ethics with Guidelines

Adopted by the ICMA membership in 1924, the
Code and Guidelines were last revised in May 1995.

The purposes of ICMA are to enhance the quality of local government and to support and assist professional local administrators in the United States and other countries. To further these objectives, certain principles, as enforced by the Rules of Procedure, shall govern the conduct of every member of ICMA, who shall:

1. Be dedicated to the concepts of effective and democratic local government by responsible elected officials and believe that professional general management is essential to the achievement of this objective.

2. Affirm the dignity and worth of the services rendered by government and maintain a constructive, creative, and practical attitude toward local government affairs and a deep sense of social responsibility as a trusted public servant.

    Guideline

    Advice to Officials of Other Local Governments. When members advise and respond to inquiries from elected or appointed officials of other local governments, they should inform the administrators of those communities.

3. Be dedicated to the highest ideals of honor and integrity in all public and personal relationships in order that the member may merit the respect and confidence of the elected officials, of other officials and employees, and of the public.

    Guidelines

    Public Confidence. Members should conduct themselves so as to maintain public confidence in their profession, their local government, and in their performance of the public trust.

    Impression of Influence. Members should conduct their official and personal affairs in such a manner as to give the clear impression that they cannot be improperly influenced in the performance of their official duties.

Appointment Commitment. Members who accept an appointment to a position should not fail to report for that position. This does not preclude the possibility of a member considering several offers or seeking several positions at the same time, but once a bona fide offer of a position has been accepted, that commitment should be honored. Oral acceptance of an employment offer is considered binding unless the employer makes fundamental changes in terms of employment.

Credentials. An application for employment should be complete and accurate as to all pertinent details of education, experience, and personal history. Members should recognize that both omissions and inaccuracies must be avoided.

Professional Respect. Members seeking a management position should show professional respect for persons formerly holding the position or for others who might be applying for the same position. Professional respect does not preclude honest differences of opinion; it does preclude attacking a person's motives or integrity in order to be appointed to a position.

Confidentiality. Members should not discuss or divulge information with anyone about pending or completed ethics cases, except as specifically authorized by the Rules of Procedure for Enforcement of the Code of Ethics.

Seeking Employment. Members should not seek employment for a position having an incumbent administrator who has not resigned or been officially informed that his or her services are to be terminated.

4.   Recognize that the chief function of local government at all times is to serve the best interests of all the people.

Guideline

Length of Service. A minimum of two years generally is considered necessary in order to render a professional service to the local government. A short tenure should be the exception rather than a recurring experience. However, under special circumstances, it may be in the best interests of the local government and the member to separate in a shorter time. Examples of such circumstances would include refusal of the appointing authority to honor commitments concerning conditions of employment, a vote of no confidence in the member, or severe personal problems. It is the responsibility of an applicant for a position to ascertain conditions of employment. Inadequately determining terms of employment prior to arrival does not justify premature termination.

5.   Submit policy proposals to elected officials; provide them with facts and advice on matters of policy as a basis for making decisions and setting community goals; and uphold and implement local government policies adopted by elected officials.

Guideline

Conflicting Roles. Members who serve multiple roles—working as both city attorney and city manager for the same community, for example—should avoid participating in matters that create the appearance of a conflict of interest. They should disclose the potential conflict to the governing body so that other opinions may be solicited.

6.   Recognize that elected representatives of the people are entitled to the credit for the establishment of local government policies; responsibility for policy execution rests with the members.

7.   Refrain from participation in the election of the members of the employing legislative body, and from all partisan political activities which would impair performance as a professional administrator.

Guidelines

Elections of the Governing Body. Members should maintain a reputation for serving equally and impartially all members of the governing body of the local government they serve, regardless of party. To this end, they should not engage in active participation in the election campaign on behalf of or in opposition to candidates for the governing body.

Elections of Elected Executives. Members should not engage in the election campaign of any candidate for mayor or elected county executive.

Other Elections. Members share with their fellow citizens the right and responsibility to exercise their franchise and voice their opinion on public issues. However, in order not to impair their effectiveness on behalf of the local government they serve, they should not participate in election campaigns for representatives from their areas to local government, school, state, and federal offices.

Elections on the Council-Manager Plan. Members may assist in preparing and presenting materials that explain the council-manager form of government to the public prior to an election on the use of the plan. If assistance is required by another community, members may respond. All activities regarding ballot issues should be conducted within local regulations and in a professional manner.

Presentation of Issues. Members may assist the governing body in presenting issues involved in referenda such as bond issues, annexations, and similar matters.

8. Make it a duty continually to improve the member's professional ability and to develop the competence of associates in the use of management techniques.

Guidelines

Self-Assessment. Each member should assess his or her professional skills and abilities on a periodic basis.

Professional Development. Each member should commit at least 40 hours per year to professional development activities that are based on the practices identified by the members of ICMA.

9. Keep the community informed on local government affairs; encourage communication between the citizens and all local government officers; emphasize friendly and courteous service to the public; and seek to improve the quality and image of public service.

10. Resist any encroachment on professional responsibilities, believing the member should be free to carry out official policies without interference, and handle each problem without discrimination on the basis of principle and justice.

Guideline

Information Sharing. The member should openly share information with the governing body while diligently carrying out the member's responsibilities as set forth in the charter or enabling legislation.

11. Handle all matters of personnel on the basis of merit so that fairness and impartiality govern a member's decisions pertaining to appointments, pay adjustments, promotions, and discipline.

Guideline

Equal Opportunity. Members should develop a positive program that will ensure meaningful employment opportunities for all segments of the community. All programs, practices, and operations should: (1) provide equality of opportunity in employment for all persons; (2) prohibit discrimination because of race, color, religion, sex, national origin, political affiliation, physical handicaps, age, or marital status; and (3) promote continuing programs of affirmative action at every level within the organization.

It should be the members' personal and professional responsibility to actively recruit and hire minorities and women to serve on professional staffs throughout their organizations.

12. Seek no favor; believe that personal aggrandizement or profit secured by confidential information or by misuse of public time is dishonest.

Guidelines

Gifts. Members should not directly or indirectly solicit any gift or accept or receive any gift—whether it be money, services, loan, travel, entertainment, hospitality, promise, or any other form—under the following circumstances: (1) it could be reasonably inferred or expected that the gift was intended to influence them in the performance of their official duties; or (2) the gift was intended to serve as a reward for any official action on their part.

It is important that the prohibition of unsolicited gifts be limited to circumstances related to improper influence. In de minimis situations such as tobacco and meal checks, for example, some modest maximum dollar value should be determined by the member as a guideline. The guideline is not intended to isolate members from normal social practices where gifts among friends, associates, and relatives are appropriate for certain occasions.

Investments in Conflict with Official Duties. Members should not invest or hold any investment, directly or indirectly, in any financial business, commercial, or other private transaction that creates a conflict with their official duties.

In the case of real estate, the potential use of confidential information and knowledge to further a member's personal interest requires special consideration. This guideline recognizes that members' official actions and decisions can be influenced if there is a conflict with personal investments. Purchases and sales which might be interpreted as speculation for quick profit ought to be avoided (see guideline on "Confidential Information").

Because personal investments may prejudice or may appear to influence official actions and decisions, members may, in concert with their governing body, provide for disclosure of such investments prior to accepting their position as local government administrator or prior to any official action by the governing body that may affect such investments.

Personal Relationships. Members should disclose any personal relationship to the governing body in any instance where there could be the appearance of a conflict of interest. For example, if the manager's spouse works for a developer doing business with the local government, that fact should be disclosed.

Confidential Information. Members should not disclose to others, or use to further their personal interest, confidential information acquired by them in the course of their official duties.

Private Employment. Members should not engage in, solicit, negotiate for, or promise to accept private employment, nor should they render services for private interests or conduct a private business when such employment, service, or business creates a conflict with or impairs the proper discharge of their official duties.

Teaching, lecturing, writing, or consulting are typical activities that may not involve conflict of interest or impair the proper discharge of their official duties. Prior notification of the appointing authority is appropriate in all cases of outside employment.

Representation. Members should not represent any outside interest before any agency, whether public or private, except with the authorization of or at the direction of the appointing authority they serve.

Endorsements. Members should not endorse commercial products or services by agreeing to use their photograph, endorsement, or quotation in paid or other commercial advertisements, whether or not for compensation. Members may, however, agree to endorse the following, provided they do not receive any compensation: (1) books or other publications; (2) professional development or educational services provided by nonprofit membership organizations or recognized educational institutions; (3) products and/or services in which the local government has a direct economic interest.

Members' observations, opinions, and analyses of commercial products used or tested by their local governments are appropriate and useful to the profession when included as part of professional articles and reports.

Reprinted with permission of ICMA, the International City/County Management Association, located in Washington, D.C.

ICMA Code of Ethics:
Rules of Procedure for Enforcement

Adopted by the ICMA Executive Board and revised in July 1992

I. General

A. These rules govern the procedures for enforcing the ICMA Code of Ethics as adopted by the ICMA membership.

B. All members of ICMA agree to abide by the Code of Ethics.

C. The purpose of these rules is to provide a reasonable process for investigating and determining whether a member has violated the code, and to afford each individual member who is the subject of an investigation (the "respondent") a full and fair opportunity to be heard throughout the process.

D. It is the intention of the ICMA membership that these rules be carried out carefully but expeditiously in order to minimize the time during which a member may be subject to possible disciplinary action. Accordingly, time limits stated in these rules are binding, subject to extensions which may be granted by the Committee on Professional Conduct (CPC), or the ICMA executive director, for reasonable cause, upon request.

E. No person may participate in any proceedings on a complaint brought under these rules if that person is or may be a witness or complainant in that case, or if his or her participation would otherwise create, or appear to create, a conflict of interests. The executive director may select a replacement for any person (other than a member of the Executive Board) who is unable to participate in the case for this reason.

II. Jurisdiction

A. All members of ICMA in active service to a local government are subject to the Code of Ethics and are subject to sanctions for any violations thereof which occur during their membership. However, elected officials are not subject to Tenet 7, and members not in service are subject only to Tenets 1 and 3. A member may be subject to sanctions for a violation which continues while he or she is a member even though the conduct in question originated prior to admission to membership.

B. If a complaint is made against a person who was a member at the time the alleged violation occurred, but who is not a member at the time the complaint is made, the complaint will be processed under these procedures only if the former member agrees in writing. In no event shall a person be readmitted to membership if there is an outstanding and unresolved complaint against him or her for conduct while formerly a member.

C. The committee shall retain jurisdiction over an investigation of a respondent who, before the conclusion of the investigation, resigns from ICMA or otherwise allows his or her membership in ICMA to lapse.

III. Responsibilities

A. The ICMA Executive Board is responsible for making the final decision on matters pertaining to the enforcement of the code, including, but not limited to, sanctions for the violation thereof. No current or former member may be publicly censured, expelled, or barred from membership without the approval of the Executive Board.

B. The Committee on Professional Conduct (CPC) is the committee of ICMA responsible for assisting the Executive Board in implementing these rules and has the specific duties set forth hereinafter.
   1. The CPC shall consist of three or more members of the ICMA Executive Board who shall be selected by the president of ICMA.
   2. CPC members shall serve for terms of one (1) year or until their successors are chosen by the president.

C. A state association consists of members of ICMA within the particular state or province. It is responsible for appointing fact-finding committees.

D. A fact-finding committee is a committee of ICMA, appointed by a state association, and is responsible for conducting the investigation of a complaint of a violation of the code in accordance with these rules. Members of a fact-finding committee shall serve until the conclusion of the investigation they were appointed to conduct, or until such later date as the state association of ICMA members may request.

E. The executive director shall assist the Executive Board and the CPC in enforcing the code and implementing these rules. It is the responsibility of the executive director to publicize the existence and importance of the code with elected officials and the general public.

1. The executive director may privately advise members on the ethical implications of their conduct under the code. However, the opinion or advice of the executive director shall not be binding on the Executive Board, the CPC, or any fact-finding committee.

2. The executive director may designate a member of the ICMA staff to carry out any of the responsibilities assigned to the executive director under these rules.

IV. Sanctions

A. Sanctions may be imposed in accordance with these rules upon members who are found to have violated the code. In determining the kind of sanction to be imposed, the following factors may be considered: the nature of the violation, prior violations by the same individual, the willfulness of the violation, the level of professional or public responsibility of the individual, and any other factors which bear upon the seriousness of the violation.

B. The following sanctions may be imposed singly or in combination at the conclusion of an investigation and/or hearing under these rules:

1. *Private Censure.* A letter to the respondent, the state association, and the complainant, indicating that the respondent has been found to have violated the Code of Ethics, that ICMA disapproves of such conduct, and that, if it is repeated in the future, it may be cause for more serious sanctions. If the complainant is a nonmember, he or she shall be notified that the case was considered and resolved, and that no public action was taken.

2. *Public Censure.* Notification to the respondent, complainant, state association, appropriate local governing bodies, and news media, indicating that a violation of the code took place and that ICMA strongly disapproves of such conduct and the nature of the sanction(s) imposed.

3. *Expulsion.* A revocation of the respondent's membership privileges.

4. *Membership Bar.* A prohibition against reinstatement of the respondent's membership in ICMA.

C. Upon receiving documented evidence that a member has been found guilty after trial by a judge or a jury of criminal conduct, which constitutes a violation of the ICMA Code of Ethics and which occurred while the person was a member of ICMA, the executive director shall immediately issue a notice of suspension of membership to that person by registered mail and that person's membership shall be suspended as of the date of that notice. The executive director shall advise the CPC of any such action and shall refer the case to the CPC. The CPC may commence an investigation in accordance with Part VI hereof, or it may defer proceedings until the person has exhausted all appeals or the time for appeal has expired. The suspension shall continue in effect until such time as sanctions provided under Part IV.B. are imposed, or the case is dismissed, in accordance with these Rules.

V. Initiation of Procedures

A. Proceedings against an individual for an alleged violation of the Code of Ethics may be initiated by the executive director upon receiving a written complaint or other written information from any source indicating that a violation may have occurred.

B. Upon receiving such a written complaint or information, the executive director must ascertain whether it is sufficiently clear and complete to initiate proceedings, and, if so, whether it alleges conduct that may be a violation of the Code of Ethics. If the executive director concludes that the complaint is not sufficiently clear or complete to initiate proceedings, he or she shall seek further clarification from the complainant or other source before taking any further action.

1. If the executive director cannot determine whether the conduct alleged, if proven, might violate the Code of Ethics, he or she shall refer the question to the CPC for a ruling. No further action shall be taken with respect to the complaint or information unless the CPC rules that the conduct alleged, if true, may constitute a violation of the code.

2. If the executive director concludes that the complaint is sufficiently clear and complete to initiate proceedings, and may, if proven, indicate a violation of the code, a copy of the complaint or information shall be forwarded by registered mail to the respondent named in the complaint or information. The respondent shall be informed at the time of the provisions of the code which he or she is alleged to have violated. The executive director may also request that the respondent answer specific questions pertaining to the alleged violation.

3. The respondent shall be given thirty (30) days within which to respond in writing to the complaint or information, to provide any further information or material he or she considers relevant to the allegations, and to answer any specific questions asked by the executive director.

4. As soon as the respondent's response is received, but in no event more than thirty (30) days after written notice of the alleged violation has been given to the respondent, the executive director shall refer the case to the CPC for proceedings in accordance with these rules.

VI. Investigations

A. Upon receiving a case of an alleged violation of the Code of Ethics from the executive director, the CPC shall commence an investigation into the allegations. However, no investigation shall be required if (1) the respondent admits to the violation in his or her initial response, or (2) the respondent has already entered a guilty plea, or has been found guilty and has exhausted all appeals, in a criminal case involving the same conduct.

B. In all cases other than those in which an investigation is not required, the executive director, at the request of the CPC, shall request the state association for the state in which the violation is alleged to have occurred to appoint an ICMA fact-finding committee to conduct the investigation. If the violation is alleged to have occurred in more than one state, at least one member of the committee shall be from the state involved. In the event that there is no active association in a state, the CPC shall appoint an ICMA fact-finding committee from one or more state(s) for this purpose.

1. The fact-finding committee shall consist of not less than three (3) ICMA members. No one other than an ICMA member may serve on the ICMA fact-finding committee.

2. A fact-finding committee must be appointed within fifteen (15) days of the request made by the executive director.

3. The fact-finding committee shall afford the respondent an opportunity to meet with the committee in person and may, at its discretion, afford such an opportunity to the complainant as well. The respondent may appear at such a meeting personally and be accompanied by a representative. Alternatively, the respondent may appear through a representative.

4. The fact-finding committee shall prepare and maintain notes of all meetings and interviews with the respondent, the complainant, and any witnesses, and may request any such person to sign a statement prepared on the basis of those notes. The respondent shall be entitled to review these notes and statements, and any other documentary evidence gathered in the course of the investigation, and shall be afforded the opportunity to respond in writing thereto.

5. The fact-finding committee shall take all reasonable steps to ascertain the facts relevant to the case, including, but not limited to, interviews with witnesses, review of the respondent's submission(s), and examination of all published material judged to be relevant and reliable.

6. Within sixty (60) days of the appointment of the fact-finding committee, the investigation shall be concluded, and a written report of the committee's proposed findings of fact shall be sent to the executive di-

rector and the respondent. Each finding must be supported by reliable and relevant evidence which has been made available to the respondent for review.

VII. Decisions

A. The CPC shall promptly review the fact-finding committee's proposed findings of fact and shall ascertain whether they are supported by sufficient reliable and relevant evidence.

1. If the evidence is not sufficient, the CPC may either (a) dismiss the case; (b) return it to the fact-finding committee for further investigation in accordance with these rules; or (c) refer the case to the Executive Board for a hearing in accordance with Part VIII of these rules.

2. If the CPC determines that the proposed findings are supported by the evidence, it shall determine whether they demonstrate that a violation of the Code of Ethics has occurred. If not, it shall dismiss the case and so advise the respondent, the fact-finding committee, the state association, and the executive director.

3. If the CPC concludes on the basis of the fact-finding committee's report that a violation has occurred, it shall determine the appropriate sanction(s). The CPC shall then notify the respondent of its intent to adopt the fact-finding committee's report as final, and to impose the specified sanction(s) for the reasons stated, unless the respondent can show that the findings of facts are erroneous, or that the proposed sanctions(s) should not be imposed in light of certain mitigating factors which the CPC did not previously consider. The respondent shall have fifteen (15) days in which to submit a written response to the CPC and/or to request a hearing.

4. In event that the respondent makes no submission, and does not request a hearing, the CPC shall promptly adopt the proposed findings and sanction(s) as final and so inform the executive director.

5. In the event that the respondent makes a written submission, but does not request a hearing, the CPC shall review the submission and may either adopt, or revise and adopt as revised, the proposed findings and/or sanction(s), as it deems appropriate. The CPC shall promptly notify the executive director of its decision.

6. In the event that the respondent requests a hearing, the CPC shall refer the case, including its recommended sanction(s), for a hearing before the Executive Board. Hearings shall be conducted in accordance with Part VIII of these rules. No sanction(s) shall be imposed before the hearing is concluded.

B. Upon receiving notice from the CPC of its determination that a private censure is the appropriate sanction, and that the respondent has not requested a hearing, the executive director shall send a letter of private censure to the respondent, with copies to the complainant and the state association. The case shall then be closed.

    1.   No other notification of a private censure shall be made. However, ICMA may publish the fact that certain kinds of conduct have resulted in the issuance of private censures, provided that no names or identifying details are disclosed.

C. Upon receiving notice from the CPC of its determination that a public censure, expulsion, or membership bar is the appropriate sanction, and that the respondent has not requested a hearing, the Executive Board may vote to adopt the recommended decision of the CPC, to modify said decision, or to dismiss the case without imposing sanctions. The respondent shall be immediately notified of the decision of the Executive Board, and the sanction, if any, shall be implemented.

VIII. Hearings

A. These procedures shall govern all hearings conducted pursuant to these rules.

B. No board member may hear any case if his or her participation in that case would create an actual or apparent conflict of interest.

C. Within ten (10) days of receiving a request for a hearing, the executive director shall notify the respondent by registered or certified mail that a hearing has been scheduled before the Executive Board. The hearing date shall be at least fifteen (15) days after the date the notice is postmarked. The notice shall also state that the respondent has the following rights:

    1.   To appear personally at the hearing;

    2.   To be accompanied and represented at the hearing by an attorney or other representative;

    3.   To review all documentary evidence, if any, against him or her, in advance of the hearing;

    4.   To cross-examine any witness who testifies against him or her at the hearing; and

    5.   To submit documentary evidence, and to present testimony, including the respondent's, in his or her defense at the hearing.

D. The Executive Board shall not be bound by any formal rules of evidence but may accord appropriate weight to the evidence based on its relevance and reliability.

1. The fact-finding committee's report shall be admissible evidence at the hearing.

2. The Executive Board may not hear evidence of any alleged ethics violation by the respondent that was not the subject of the initial investigation.

E. At any hearing conducted under these rules, the CPC shall first present evidence in support of its recommended decision. Upon conclusion of its presentation, the respondent shall have the opportunity to present evidence in his or her defense.

F. Within five (5) working days of the conclusion of the hearing, the Executive Board shall render a decision in the case.

1. The decision shall be in writing and shall include a statement of the reasons therefore. Only evidence which was put before the Executive Board may be considered as a basis for the decision.

2. The Executive Board's decision may be to:
   a. Dismiss the case;
   b. Adopt the findings and sanction(s) recommended by the CPC; or
   c. Revise, and adopt as revised, the findings and/or sanction(s) recommended by the CPC. However, the Executive Board may not increase the sanction(s) recommended by the CPC unless new evidence, not previously available to the CPC, is disclosed at the hearing, which indicates that the respondent's violation was more serious. No sanction may be imposed for any violation of which the respondent had no prior notice.

3. A copy of the written decision of the Executive Board shall be sent immediately by registered mail to the respondent, the Executive Board, the CPC, the state association, and the executive director.

4. Promptly after receiving a copy of the written decision, the executive director shall implement the sanction(s), if any, imposed by the Executive Board in accordance with the rules.

Code of Ethics for [N.C.] School Board Members

As a member of my local board of education I will strive to improve public education, and to that end I will:

Attend all regularly scheduled board meetings insofar as possible, and become informed concerning the issues to be considered at those meetings;

Recognize that I should endeavor to make policy decisions only after full discussion at publicly held board meetings;

Render all decisions based on the available facts and my independent judgment, and refuse to surrender that judgment to individuals or special interest groups;

Encourage the free expression of opinion by all board members, and seek systematic communications between the board and students, staff, and all elements of the community;

Work with other board members to establish effective board policies and to delegate authority for the administration of the schools to the superintendent;

Communicate to other board members and the superintendent expressions of public reaction to board policies and school programs;

Inform myself about current educational issues by individual study and through participation in programs providing needed information, such as those sponsored by my state and national school boards associations;

Support the employment of those persons best qualified to serve as school staff, and insist on a regular and impartial evaluation of all staff;

Avoid being placed in a position of conflict of interest, and refrain from using my board position for personal or partisan gain;

Take no private action that will compromise the board or administration, and respect the confidentiality of information that is privileged under applicable law; and

Remember always that my first and greatest concern must be the educational welfare of the students attending the public schools.

_____

Board Member Signature

_____

Date

Source: North Carolina School Boards Association